THE CROSS AS A TREE

THE CROSS AS A TREE

*Themes of Interest to
the Company of Phurah*

by

PERCY W. EVANS, D.D.
Principal of Spurgeon's College

MARSHALL, MORGAN & SCOTT LTD.
LONDON :: EDINBURGH

MARSHALL, MORGAN & SCOTT LTD.
LONDON :: EDINBURGH

U.S.A.
ZONDERVAN PUBLISHING HOUSE
847 OTTAWA AVE., N.W.
GRAND RAPIDS
MICHIGAN

CANADA
EVANGELICAL PUBLISHERS
366 BAY STREET
TORONTO

First published 1946

*This book is produced
in complete conformity
with the authorized economy standards*

MADE AND PRINTED IN GREAT BRITAIN BY
MORRISON AND GIBB LTD., LONDON AND EDINBURGH

FOREWORD

MOST of the contents of this book first appeared in *The Christian*, and were intended for such people as are described in the first chapter—men and women serving the cause of Christ as Phurah served Gideon. In every Church they are the majority, and to them, under God, the persistence and effectiveness of the Churches are due. They usually lack the technical knowledge of the professional theologian, but they possess the power, the right and the duty to form theological judgments. Their loyalty to Christ sometimes enables them to reach the heart of a controversy, even though ignorant of its complex details, and it is Christian statesmanship to consider their verdict and to provide them with some materials for arriving at it.

As successive articles appeared, correspondence developed a real fellowship between the writer and his readers, to which the title " The Company of Phurah " was given. The author gratefully acknowledges his debt to these correspondents for their helpful suggestions and encouragement and—especially—for their generous openness of mind.

The type of theology represented in these pages would be called conservative; that epithet needs no apology to-day when Britain makes incalculable sacrifices that she may preserve her ancient dower. Theology, however, must be dealt with by the conservative as the Thames Conservators deal with the river of which they have charge—preserving its waters from impurities, guarding its banks, but always regarding it as a river, not a reservoir. It is an honourable task to strive to defend Christian truth alike from contamination and stagnation, remembering always that the worst harm comes, not from doctrinal error but from any kind of unfairness or uncharitableness. The writer hopes that in these pages he has avoided that peril.

SPURGEON'S COLLEGE,
LONDON.

5

CONTENTS

CONTENTS

I

INTRODUCING PHURAH

HE needs introduction. He was never assertive or pushful, and in a world that values " drive " he could not be prominent or famous. He utterly lacked the gift of advertising, so that self-made men who judge merit by applause could almost overlook his very existence. Only once is he mentioned in the holy records, and even there the Authorised and Revised Versions disagree over the spelling of his name; in the R. V. he is merely " Purah ". We use the longer form of the older version, in the hope that its familiarity may help us to greater familiarity with an insufficiently recognised hero.

In Judg. vii. 10 and 11, the whole known history of Phurah is told, and unless we are prepared to bring sympathetic imagination to the narrative we shall miss the wonder of it. Here is the warrior whose name everyone knows—Gideon, with exploits already to his credit, with a faith in God that makes him ready to dispense with the big battalions. Gideon has the skill of the general and the personal courage of the soldier; he needs it when he is commanded by God to go—without even the three hundred—into the camp of the enemy. A perilous journey, which at first glance looks like a reckless exposure of the pivotal man to danger ! Brave as they are, we do not permit our supreme commanders thus to hazard their lives. At that time no rules of war secured honourable captivity for an enemy general taken prisoner; if Gideon were discovered, death would be his lot, and that would involve discouragement and defeat for Israel. All this risk had to be taken and faced in the darkness of the night. It is not surprising that the divine voice speaks of the possibility of fear, but fear grows in solitude, therefore companionship is given. " If thou fear to go down, go thou with Phurah thy servant." He availed himself of this supporting comradeship, went down with Phurah to the camp, heard the dream which gave promise and evidence of coming victory, and then returned with hands and heart strengthened. That courage and hope would apparently have been withheld had not the companionship of Phurah been given to Gideon in the midnight hour and the dangerous adventure.

Then Phurah disappears from the story altogether. He is called Gideon's servant; we may think of him as a young man, whom later times would call an armour-bearer; but whatever his occupation he is clearly marked out as a man for secondary tasks. Did he possess great courage of his own? Probably not, but he could be an essential ingredient in another man's heroism. Without the gift of initiating, he yet had the qualities that make for co-operation. There must have been discipline in the man, for apparently he had passed the test that eliminated the crowd, and he was left among the three hundred. Yet he is follower rather than commander, not born for single-handed exploits, but an accomplice in someone else's endeavours, an accompanist of other people's solos. He may be secondary in rank, but is he not of first-rate importance?

We who know that we shall never resemble Gideon ought to be lovers and imitators of Phurah, for in many ways his service is greater than that of his famous leader. That may be comparing dissimilar things, but at least Gideon owes much to Phurah, and if a new order were to be founded it might well be named " The Company of Phurah ". It would include the noble army of missionary givers and intercessors, the unseen loyalists who maintain prominent Christian activities, in the report of which their names seldom, if ever, appear. They are apt to be included in a perfunctory " etc."; their names are not in the style of the firm but are hidden in the addendum " & Co.". We frequently see Phurah and his company standing around the speakers and singers at an open-air meeting. They do not give addresses, and their voices are only useful in the chorus, but they stand there identifying themselves with the cause of the Gospel, braving the amused stare of the passers-by; if they do sing any solo, it is a song within the heart, and the words are something like this: " I'm not ashamed to own my Lord! "

When Phurah comes to any place of worship he makes the sermon far more effective, yet never knows what he has done. A congregation of Phurahs would make a " stickit minister " into an eloquent evangelist. C. H. Spurgeon had a devoted follower who delighted to call himself the great preacher's " armour-bearer ", but all ministers whose word God has blessed owe much to people of this group, whether they are called armour-bearers or Phurahs—but the latter name is better.

Phurah—not Pharaoh ! The humble colleague has nothing in common with the proud monarch, but the Bible names many Pharaohs and only one Phurah. And in these days we can be thankful that Phurah is not Fuehrer ! What a suggestive marginal reading is that in 2 John, 9 : " *Whosoever taketh the lead* and abideth not in the teaching of Christ hath not God ". If we seek the Fuehrer we can discover him in 3 John, 9 : " Diotrephes, who loveth to have the pre-eminence."

Did Gideon know how much he owed to Phurah ? When he told the story afterwards did he omit his companion's name ? We could measure his true greatness better if we knew whether he said " we went " or " I went ". The grandeur of Paul comes out in his habit of including other people with himself in salutations and exhortations. He is no monopolist, anxious to secure all the glory for himself. That lovely quality the Apostle surely learnt from his Lord. Have you noticed that Christ, Who is not ashamed to call us brethren, associates us with Himself, unimportant as we are ? " *We* must work the works of Him that sent Me." He never forgets the company of Phurah.

Is not the Church largely composed of Phurah and his like ? " Not many mighty, not many wise, not many rich " ; an early opponent, Celsus, compared the Church to " a congregation of frogs croaking in a swamp ". But Christ is not ashamed of them.

We believe that Phurah can be discovered in the New Testament as well as in the Old. One day two people went towards Emmaus ; they discussed the Scriptures and the latest great happening. One was apparently the leader, for his name is mentioned ; was the other a quiet listener, without striking ideas of his own ? He had one characteristic—his heart was cold, and the fact grieved him. Presently the Third came, and in His company the Scripture and the novel tidings the women had brought were fused together in one glowing Gospel, and the hearts that had been cold were now burning. We know the Third; who were the other two? Luke calls one of them Cleopas, but does not tell us the name of the other. Could it have been—Phurah?

II

THE CROSS AS A TREE

An event so wonderful as the Crucifixion inevitably appeals to varied aspects of different minds. Its meaning touches the conscience and the will, effecting moral transformation; it challenges and also enlarges thought, creating Christian theology; it appeals to the imagination, quickening the genius of artist and poet, and not only the imagination of these but also that of the evangelist, so that he uses a multitude of symbols and metaphors to express what is too marvellous to be fully stated in one prosaic fashion. We can see this process at work in the New Testament in the fact that, whilst historians and writers of epistles know and employ the Greek word for the Cross, they often speak and think of it as a tree. The wealth of suggestion in that usage is worth studying.

Peter has the habit; he accuses the Sanhedrim of responsibility for the death of Jesus, " whom ye slew, hanging Him on a tree " (Acts v. 30), and repeats the statement and the phrase in the house of Cornelius (Acts x. 39). Did Paul catch the phrase from Peter? From Gal. i. 18 we learn that the purpose of his first visit to Jerusalem after his conversion was " to become acquainted with Peter " ; Dr. Lukyn Williams says that the word suggests " that St. Paul's visit to Jerusalem was prompted more by curiosity to see St. Peter than by any other motive ". We often and naturally think of Paul influencing Peter, that receptive personality, but the influence would be mutual, and we may discover a slight trace of it in the fact that in the first recorded Pauline sermon (Acts xiii. 29) he speaks of the Cross as " the tree ". A further reference by Peter is, of course, to be found in 1 Pet. ii. 24 : " He Himself bore our sins in His own body on (perhaps " up on to ") the tree ".

Why " tree " instead of " cross " ? " Cross " suggested intense suffering, but since it was a Roman method of punishment it might be inflicted on those whom the subject people would regard as national heroes; it might not in every case,

therefore, carry the connotation of " shame ", though admittedly that would often be there. For a Jew, however,
Deut. xxi. 23 gave to the word " tree " exactly the association
of degrading humiliation, and—more than that—the suggestion of " the curse ". " He that is hanged is accursed of
God." Moffatt's version is " An impaled man is under
God's curse ". We must notice here that the action forbidden
is not that of causing death by crucifixion, but of hanging
upon a tree one who has *previously* (and, presumably, by
some other method) been put to death. The exposure of the
dead body, instead of its decent interment, is thus linked in
the Hebrew mind with Divine malediction. Confessedly, it
is very difficult, if we take the Deuteronomy passage alone, to
see how what happened to a man's body after his death could
in and of itself bring him under the curse of God; on the
other hand, it is to be remembered that the man in his lifetime
had " committed a sin worthy of death "; it would be more
natural to assume that the " curse " follows upon his sin,
not upon the manner of disposal of his corpse. Presently
we shall consider the use made of this passage in Gal. iii. 13,
but before doing so it may be worth while to cite the note
by Dr. C. H. Waller on the Deuteronomy passage. He quotes
the Jewish commentator Rashi (of the eleventh century) as
saying : " He that is hanged is the curse of God (see margin),
—that is, he is *the King's disgrace*. For man was made in the
likeness of His image, and Israel are His children. There
were two twin brothers who were much alike. One was made
king, the other was taken up for highway robbery, and was
hanged. Everyone who saw him said, ' There hangs the
king ! ' " Rashi seems to imply that the hanging was a
disgrace to *God*, since it was maltreatment of man made in
the Divine image.

Now, in Gal. iii. 13 St. Paul quotes this Deuteronomic
verse from the Greek version in these words: " Cursed is
everyone that hangeth upon a tree ". The " curse ", however,
which Paul believes our Lord bore for us is not merely or
mainly the manner of His death, but is indicated in the earlier
passage quoted from Deuteronomy in the same chapter of
Gal. (iii. 10): " Cursed is everyone which continueth not in
all things that are written in the book of the law, to do them "

(Deut. xxvii. 26). In other words, Paul cites Deut. xxi. 23 not to provide himself with an argument but as furnishing a striking expression of the fact of " the curse ", the curse being the consequence of the broken law, not the malefactor's shameful death. There is undoubtedly in our Lord's death the bearing of something which we can only designate as " the curse ", but it follows from the connection of His death with sin, not from what men did with " His body, broken in our stead ". Naturally, however, when men were reminded that the Old Testament linked the hanging of a body on the tree with the idea of a curse, the association of ideas was strengthened, and " tree " stood for " curse ". Dr. Vincent Taylor, in *The Atonement in New Testament Teaching* (p. 128), insists that " a spiritual experience of reprobation is meant, and since this cannot be personal, it must be participation in the reprobation which rests upon sin ". Elsewhere he well says: " In perfect filial accord with the Father's will, and moved by the greatness of His love for sinners, Christ came under the curse of sin and shared its penalty ".

Suffering, shame, curse—these do not exhaust the suggestiveness of " the tree ". Inevitably there occurs to the mind the contrast between " that forbidden tree, whose mortal taste Brought death into the world and all our woe, With loss of Eden ", and this Tree of Life. In an apocryphal writing called " The Gospel of Nicodemus or Acts of Pilate " Hades, which has lost its captives through the victory of Christ, reproaches Satan, saying: " O prince Satan, holder of the keys of hell, those thy riches which thou hadst gained by the tree of transgression and the losing of paradise, thou hast lost by the tree of the Cross, and all thy gladness hath perished. When thou didst hang up Christ Jesus the King of glory thou wroughtest against thyself and me ". Again, the Cross is a tree like that which at Marah (Ex. xv. 25) made the bitter waters sweet; " Here earth's precious things seem dross, Here earth's bitter things grow sweet ".

Fruitfulness is an idea inseparable from the thought of a tree, and so the conqueror is promised access to and partaking of " the tree of life, which is in the midst of the Paradise of God " (Rev. ii. 7), whilst on each side of the river of the water of life is " the tree of life, bearing twelve kinds (or " crops ") of fruit, yielding its fruit every month, and the leaves of the tree were for the healing of the nations ".

The extending branches of a tree make it yet further a fit symbol of the Cross. Joseph is (in Gen. xlix. 22) called " a fruitful bough by a well, whose branches run over the wall ". The spreading arms of the Cross of our Lord Jesus Christ have typified for devout believers the all-including love of the Crucified Himself, a love which knew no racial, social or intellectual limitations. Like the fruitful trees, its ministry grew beyond the narrow confines of Judaism. Above all the dividing walls men can build, the wide-branching Cross still rises. It is a tree that the small tidy gardens of the different Churches and Christian communions cannot monopolise. In a day of separation between nations, we rejoice in that Tree of Life whose branches run over all the walls and whose fruit is for the healing of the nations.

Let us gather up the manifold meanings: suffering, shame and curse; life, fruitfulness, expansion; and there is yet one more—sovereignty. The Tree is a throne. To Ps. xcvi. 10 some MSS of the Septuagint version add certain words, so that the verse reads: " the Lord reigned from the tree ". The authority for this is not any manuscript or other textual evidence; the idea, though not the words, can be discovered in what actually happened at the Crucifixion. The Lord, majestic amid suffering, promised a place in His kingdom to the dying thief, and on the tree where they thought to destroy Him He reigned as King !

The Cross as a Tree—the symbol is rich, but the truth is richer far !

III

THE PRIESTHOOD OF ALL BELIEVERS

WAS Phurah a priest? We have regarded him as repre-
sentative of the noble fellowship of unnamed servants of God,
but as we do not know to what tribe he belonged we cannot
say whether he is to be classed among what our imperfect
phrases describe as " clergy or laity ", " priests or people ".
From the New Testament standpoint, however, we can boldly
declare that every Phurah (in the sense here intended) is of
the priestly tribe, for he shares in " The Priesthood of all
Believers ". He—or *she*!—for since in Christ " there is
neither male nor female ", the sex barrier does not operate in
this realm !

The priesthood of all believers has since Reformation days
been a cardinal doctrine common to all Protestants. It is
easy for phrases to do duty for thought, however, and it may
well be helpful to look again at what is intended by the words;
battle-cries that roused one generation to conflict and victory
may degenerate into slogans which we automatically applaud,
and finally become narcotics which dull the mind.

The most impressive statement of the doctrine of the
priesthood of all believers was, of course, made in the sixteenth
century, when the evils of the monopolist priesthood became
horribly plain to awakened men and women; they rebelled
against the false limitation of priesthood to an officially-
appointed class, a limitation which a modern Protestant
denounced in strong but justified words when he said: " The
sacerdotal syndicates affirm that what cannot be done by
the best of men outside their circle can be done with ease by
the worst of men within their pale ".

Before we consider the Reformers' statement of the doctrine,
let us remember its Scriptural foundation. So many associations of fraud and falsity have gathered around official priest-
hoods that the word " priest " and the idea it suggests have
become laden with a certain natural prejudice, but abuse
must not blind us to the truth and beauty of priesthood. The

2

New Testament no less than the Old Testament is a priestly book. In the Old Testament there are three types of priesthood: the general priesthood of the whole people, the specialised priesthood of the tribe of Levi and the solitary priesthood of Aaron and his successors in the High Priesthood. Bible students will notice that in the Pentateuch we read of the priesthood of the whole people (in Ex. xix. 6: " Ye shall be unto me a kingdom of priests ") before any mention is made of the separation of one tribe for the office. The verse just quoted is the first mention in the Bible of any *Israelite* priesthood, and it claims the glorious title and function for the whole redeemed people. Delivered out of " the house of bondage ", every ex-slave is appointed a priest ! All the redeemed are priests, all the priests are redeemed ! It does not follow, however, that a universal privilege and possibility would always be wisely exercised universally, and since the people of Israel had the ordinary duties of life to perform it was well that some should be set apart who should concentrate upon priestly functions, which they performed however as representatives of the whole people. Out of the priestly nation, therefore, God selected the priestly tribe, without depriving the nation of its priestly character. So, to use a New Testament analogy, every Christian has the privilege and the possibility of witnessing to his Lord, but certain forms of witness, such as preaching and missionary service, are necessarily undertaken by some who fulfil these offices as representatives of their brethren. The occupant of the pulpit who realises this says " We " rather than " I ", and is upheld by the knowledge that his personal testimony is strengthened and endorsed by the consent of the listening believers. And there is one sacred moment when every Christian, official or unofficial, preacher or listener, exercises the duty of the herald; it is when, at the Table of the Lord, every communicant (not the administrator of the rite only) declares the Lord's death and announces His return. " *YE* do proclaim the Lord's death till He come ".

It is agreed by all Christians that the solitary office of the Aaronic High Priest is, under the New Covenant, fulfilled by Christ alone, but what corresponds in the New Testament Church to the two other types of priesthood ? Representatives all too often exceed their authority and misuse their office, and we all know how the special priesthood gradually usurped prominence until the general priesthood of the holy people was forgotten or suppressed. The Jewish priesthood was foremost in bringing about the crucifixion of our Lord, and therefore in the New Testament Church nothing corresponding to it can be found. The universal priesthood reappears (cf. 1 Pet. ii. 5, 9, and Rev. i. 6). This priesthood is not one of sacrifice, however, save in a metaphorical sense; the only sacrifices which Christians offer are " sacrifices of praise ", the doing of good and the yielding up of the body as " a living sacrifice " (Heb. xiii. 15, 16; Rom. xii. 1). Of course there is specialisation of function, but not limitation of priestly standing. Priesthood implies the right of access to the presence of God, and this is made possible for all believers, as the rending of the Temple veil showed. The writer to the Hebrews therefore uses the plural verb in saying: " Let *us* come with boldness to the throne of grace " (iv. 16). The gift of the Holy Spirit to all believers, without distinction of age, rank or sex (Acts ii. 17, 18) indicates that their priesthood is equally universal and without limitation.

There is a spiritual lethargy to which we are all prone, and as the centuries passed it became easier to delegate tasks to others, particularly when such tasks made a spiritual demand. (What a book might be written on the evils wrought to the Christian Church by the idea of proxies, deputies, substitutes, in matters where personal decision is imperative !) These evils culminated in the Reformation age, when Luther attacked the underlying error in his book entitled, *The Liberty of a Christian Man*. The priesthood of all believers results for Luther from the fact of justification by faith alone. Everything a man has can be traced back to faith and comes from faith. " By the use of these words, *priests*, *clergy*, *spiritual person*, *ecclesiastic*, an injustice has been done, since they have been transferred from the remaining body of Christians to those few who are now, by a hurtful custom, called ecclesiastics." Of course Luther sensibly recognised that differentiation of function to which we have referred, saying, " Though it is true that we are all equally priests, yet cannot we, nor ought we if we could, all to minister and teach publicly ",

Nevertheless " A cobbler belongs to the spiritual estate as truly as a bishop ". It was this truth that shattered the spiritual power and monopoly of the Pope. Christ is the only Mediator, and all other priests, in the exclusive sense, are dispensed with. Lindsay quotes Luther's vivid and moving words about the Communion Service: " We all kneel beside (the Priest or minister) and around him, men and women, young and old, master and servant, mistress and maid, all holy priests together, sanctified by the blood of Christ. We are there in our priestly dignity. . . . We do not let the priest proclaim for himself the ordinance of Christ; but he is the mouthpiece of us all, and we all say it with him in our hearts with true faith in the Lamb of God Who feeds us with His Body and Blood." That, says Lindsay, " is the outstanding difference between the followers of the reformed and the mediaeval religion ".

Israel Zangwill has a story of a Jew named Cohen (=priest) who had forgotten all the implications of his ancestral religion, but wished to marry the daughter of an orthodox Jew. The father of the girl forbade the marriage since she was divorced and a member of the priestly tribe must not marry such a one. He was nominally a priest and thought nothing of it. A neglected priesthood meant a forfeited joy. Are we missing yet higher joys for ourselves and others because we have forgotten our priestly standing? " He hath made us a kingdom of priests unto His God and Father ".

IV

ABOUT CONCORDANCES

In the Company of Phurah we ought certainly to include
the makers of Concordances. What should we do without
their labours ? In the realm of the Bible we should wander
as in a mighty forest, where magnificent trees awaken our
admiration but where paths intersect without distinguishing
marks, so that we are lost in the maze. The authors of
Concordances to the Scriptures come to us as guides and
helpers, not sparing us the traversing of the ways, any more
than Phurah exempted Gideon from his midnight journey,
but pointing out where the paths lead and accompanying us.

How did early students of the Scriptures manage without
Concordances ? Before such books could be made most
serviceable the division of the Scriptures into chapters and
verses was necessary, and it was not till 1545 that Robert
Stephens, a Paris printer of Huguenot sympathies, gave us
our present verse-divisions. The chapter divisions are assigned
by some to Stephen Langton, Archbishop of Canterbury from
A.D. 1207 to 1228. The first Concordance (based on the
Latin Vulgate) is traditionally ascribed to Antony of Padua,
who belongs to the same period as Stephen Langton, but
how did he refer to the various passages ?

In the early Christian centuries there is evidence of an
exact acquaintance with the words of Scripture that puts
many of us modern believers to shame. The early Fathers
cite parallel passages with wonderful accuracy, and there is
the notable case of Didymus of Alexandria, blind from six
years of age, of whom Dr. Swete said that " his writings
shew an intimate acquaintance with the contents of the Old
and New Testaments which would be surprising even in one
who had the use of his eyes ". He paid close attention to
what was read to him by others, and his trained and dis-
ciplined memory was his only Concordance. There were
other devices, however, to aid those whose keener sight was
not accompanied by an equally retentive memory. Ammonius

of Alexandria, in the third century, divided St. Matthew
into sections and then put side by side with each section its
parallel in the other Gospels. In the fourth century Eusebius
of Caesarea improved on this arrangement by dividing the
four Gospels into " sections ", or paragraphs, each containing
a single theme; there were 335 in Matthew, 233 in Mark,
342 in Luke and 232 in John. He then drew up ten lists
showing what passages in any one Gospel had parallels in
any of the others. Thus a Concordance of paragraphs was
provided, but it was to the Gospels only. It was a kind of
subject index, of limited use, but of great value in the absence
of anything better.

Concordances of the modern type, giving chapter and
verse references, begin during the sixteenth century, but there
were attempts at such work earlier. In the thirteenth century
Cardinal Hugo is said to have employed 500 monks on the
task, and there is a tradition that a Greek named George
Sugdures worked thirty years on a Greek Concordance of
the whole Bible—and then never published it! What tragedy
lies behind that story ? Was it wasted time and labour ?
Before we say, " To what purpose was this waste ? " we ought
to realise that such long and loving toil could not fail to
enrich the compiler, even if it profited no one else. And
have we the vision to count thirty years of intensive Bible
Study well spent, even if we never publish anything about it ?
Would not our lives publish something of supreme worth ?

Concordances in the Biblical languages, Hebrew, Greek
and Latin, have of course been issued, but our interest is
mainly in Concordances prepared for the English reader.
Here the familiar and still-honoured name is that of Alexander
Cruden, whose work was first published in 1737. Let me
recommend to you the words of his Dedication: " All other
books are of little or no importance in comparison with the
Holy Scriptures ". Cruden's work occupied many laborious
days, and he only permitted himself four or five hours' sleep,
but he must have felt amply repaid when he could say: " I
was told by an eminent minister that the Bible and this
Concordance taught him to preach ". Cruden was from
time to time under restraint as a person of unsound mind,
and was certainly highly eccentric, yet this crack-brained man

has been the helper of a multitude of scholarly students of Scripture. What unlikely instruments God can employ! We eminently sane people are debtors to a poet intermittently mad whenever we sing " Hark, my soul, it is the Lord " ; we read the epistles of a writer to whom it was said " Paul, thou art ' beside thyself ' " ; most of all, we are the redeemed servants of One Who " was charged with madness here ". So the foolishness of God is wiser than the wisdom of men. And it is a gladdening fact that this apparently crazed compiler of a Concordance was one of the first to visit felons in prison, that he was an assiduous tract-distributor, and that he died kneeling in prayer. These are marks of the most important kind of sanity.

So useful were Scripture Concordances found to be, that a Concordance Society now exists to aid the preparation of similar guides to standard authors. A Shakespeare Concordance took its authoress sixteen years to make, and twelve years to copy out. Nowadays such work is done co-operatively; for instance, the last Wordsworth Concordance was the work of many collaborators, each one receiving only from one-fortieth to one-eightieth of the work to do; even so, the work occupied seven months. How did the early Concordance-makers achieve so much single-handed? And why did they take such trouble?

Here is the challenge the Concordance brings! Cruden and his brethren by their devoted toil witness to an estimate of the Bible that makes its details important and its words significant in a superlative degree. They manifest their faith that the various writings from different pens composed through several centuries have a unity that is more than a mere verbal agreement. For a Bible Concordance is not merely an index by which we can find the verse we want, as we look up addresses in a directory. It is rather a means for comparing one phrase with another and for tracing the growth and development of its meaning. A Concordance thus used is a commentary and a lexicon. There are Concordances to the Bible because the Bible is concordant with itself. Concordances to Shakespeare, Milton, Wordsworth, Browning and Tennyson are compiled because in each case the work of a single author is being dealt with, and the unity of authorship makes it valuable to compare the uses by the same mind of the same word. And there is a unity of authorship in the Bible in virtue of which, while acknowledging the differing gifts of the different writers, we discover one voice speaking through many voices, and the words of the various writers become the Word of God. The agreement of the words is the result of the concord of the Word, not mere chance coincidence. The Scriptures are one in the unity of their purpose, and in the oneness of that Divine Spirit Who speaks throughout them.

What then shall be our prayer as we use our Concordance? First, thanksgiving for the Book that is opened up for us by it; then, the resolve so to hide God's Word in our hearts that our memory may become to us a partial Concordance; and finally, a petition that our life may be concordant with the will of God.

V

THE ANCIENT THRONE OF TRUTH

THE pulpit, said Edward Irving, is " the ancient throne of truth in this realm ". Irving's language, like his whole demeanour, was always lofty and majestic; is there anything of exaggerated majesty in this phrase ? We do not think so, for George Herbert, whose speech never over-strains truth, also grandly described the Christian preacher as " the deputy of Christ for the reducing of men to the obedience of God ".

That estimate must be revived among speakers and listeners if we are to have a proper view of the importance of preaching. Sixty years ago Austin Phelps said that " a sliding scale might be constructed by which one might gauge the degree of corruption in the Church of the middle ages by the progressive decline of the pulpit. No matter whether the Church succumbed to paganism or to philosophy, the result was the same; the pulpit succumbed proportionately." We must therefore magnify the preaching office. Yet we remember hearing a minister criticised because he inaugurated his ministry by preaching about Paul's word in Rom. xi. 13: " I magnify mine office " ; the choice of the text was supposed to indicate arrogance and personal pride ! It was a misunderstanding, for we all have need of the Pauline attitude in this matter.

What do his words mean ? The various renderings given are suggestive. Wade has " I make much of my ministry " ; Moffatt puts, " I lay great stress on my office " ; Sanday and Headlam suggest " I do all I can to glorify my ministry " ; Weymouth is not so good as usual with his rendering, " I take pride in my ministry " ; perhaps best of all is A. S. Way's version, " I insist upon the grandeur of my function ". My dissatisfaction with Weymouth's phrase is because it seems to make the possession of an office a reason for personal pride, whereas, rightly understood, nothing takes the conceit out of a preacher so much as to " insist upon the grandeur of his function ". Paul's emphasis is upon the office, not the official.

First of all, of course, the grandeur of the preacher's function is derived from the wonder of the message he delivers and the Lord Who commissioned him to declare it. It is worth while, however, to consider reasons on a lower level which may lead us to revive the somewhat contemptuous attitude of many moderns to the pulpit and its task. A few years ago attention was called by G. R. Owst to the historical importance of preaching. He pointed out that the older style of history dealt mainly with " treaties, campaigns and royal escapades "; that has been replaced by histories dealing more with the employments of ordinary people in the daily round, the common task. Dr. Owst urged (and his book proved) that sermon literature was an almost unrivalled mirror of human life. Quoting Pater's dictum that " nothing which has ever interested living men and women can ever lose its vitality ", he showed how the English pulpit in the middle ages gripped the men of its day. Newspapers, political meetings and parliamentary debates in normal times afford an opportunity for the expression of opinion and the airing of grievances; before these existed, their function was often partly fulfilled by the sermon. Of course, attendance at sermons was then so customary that it was almost compulsory; to-day no constraint is upon the listener, and he comes voluntarily. It is therefore the more possible that the sermon, though it has a smaller audience, may be of still greater influence.

We write especially with the thought of the unsuitably-named " local preacher " in mind. These Christian men go forth to a glorious but difficult task in circumstances that may cause the maximum of discouragement. Other preachers have advantages of which they are, by their very devotion to a special task, deprived—such as the advantage of continuity of ministry. Do we and they sufficiently remember that the sermon may be a historical turning-point ? The movement begun in the soul of one listener may become a world-revolution !

In the middle ages it was considered mortal sin for a layman to preach; we have escaped from that bondage ! Yet in the fourteenth century, under the influence of the Lollards, lay folk, men and even women, are stated to have begun to spread the word of God, shaming thus their careless clergy. In the manuscript sermons and other documents which Dr. Owst studied he found abundant complaints about unworthy and neglectful shepherds of souls, but it is refreshing to discover traces of some who were alive to the evil of the Church of their day and did what they could to correct it. Some of them were preaching friars, and Bunyan's biographer, Dr. John Brown of Bedford, was inclined to describe them as Puritan preachers before Puritan times. He may well be right; at any rate, we can rejoice in men of any name or in any age who do the work of the evangelist. Some, however, attempted to win pulpit fame by cheap methods; little books were published which gave the lazy or incompetent preacher outlines for sermons. One such book was called " Dormi Secure " (that is, " sleep quietly ") for by its aid the unready man might sleep soundly on Saturday nights ! Yet is there any place where the second-hand, the borrowed, is more mercilessly revealed than in the pulpit ?

Dr. Owst emphasises that one of the great services Wyclif rendered to preaching was his insistence on " the naked text ". Apparently a great deal of extraneous matter had clustered round the proper Biblical themes, so that some preachers entertained their hearers with marvellous stories and even broad jests, all told with an eye to the collection afterwards to be made. Let us insist upon the grandeur of our function by refusing to depart from the word of God ! Many odd requests are made of the pulpit from time to time; the author has been asked to preach about allotments, savings clubs, and the use of the humane killer in slaughter-houses ! He answered each time in the spirit, though not in the words, of Nehemiah (iv. 3): " I am doing a great work, so that I cannot *come down* ". Even if the themes suggested had been of vastly greater importance, to desert Scripture for them is " to come down ".

In mediaeval times, it appears that more women than men were found in the preacher's audience, so that one matter has not greatly changed. There are complaints of sleeping and snoring in sermon-time, of a hum of conversation drown ing the preacher's voice, and even of the playing of games during the church-service. One preacher says that the Queen of Sheba and other Christian nations will rise up in judgment against the English, because there can scarcely be found a Christian nation which so rarely and unwillingly hears the word of God !

Preaching will never be without difficulties, but the word of the Master to His servant is ever the same, " My grace is sufficient for thee ! " The day of the preacher is not over, and will not be over till the day of grace is ended ! Are there not some readers who have deprived themselves of " the grandeur of this function " by not heeding the divine call to the work ? What is the call to preach ? Ion Keith Falconer's definition cannot be bettered: " A call is a need made known, and the ability to answer that need ". Stir up the gift that is in you, make trial of your gifts and opportunities, and you may gladly discover that it is your Lord's will that you should speak for Him from " the ancient throne of truth in this realm ".

VI

WHEN DID PREACHING BEGIN ?

TIMOTHY RICHARD, that great apostle to China, told of a
notable victory he once gained in argument with a Chinaman.
Richard had spoken of the railway, the telegraph and other
Western achievements, but the Chinaman claimed that his
own country had possessed them before they were known to
the West. (Is this so, by the way, with regard to the railway ?)
Then said Richard, referring to the influence of such men as
Moody and Spurgeon, " Do you know anything of men
listening to a man for half-an-hour, and having their whole
life altered by that half-hour ? " " No ", said the Chinaman.
" We know nothing of that."

Yet this is the recurring event in Christianity. From the
beginning it has been a preaching religion, a religion that
spreads through preaching, a religion that works the marvel
of turning most unlikely people into preachers, and makes
them such preachers that listeners find the whole of life
altered. John Ruskin spoke of the preacher's opportunity
as " half-an-hour to raise the dead in ! " There are periods
of greater and lesser success, and it is sadly obvious that to-
day is not an era of such evident triumph as marked the times
of Moody and Spurgeon, Wesley and Whitefield, and the rest
of the shining company. It would be an error to suppose,
though, that preaching to-day is altogether ineffective; the
harvest ripens perhaps more slowly and less abundantly than
in former years, but it ripens ! In 1 Tim. iii. 16 the " great
open secret of our religion " includes among its great assertions
concerning Him Who was manifested in flesh not only that
He was received up in glory but that " He appeared to
messengers, He was proclaimed among the nations, He was
believed on in the world ". (" Angels " may just as well be
rendered " messengers ", and the context makes that translation more probable.) Christ still manifests Himself to those
who are to be His messengers, they still go forth preaching,

and through their preaching all sorts and conditions of men throughout the world believe on Him.

That a religion should depend upon preaching for its spread is commonly taken for granted, but is there not more in the fact than we usually realise ? In a museum in the Rhineland there is a reconstruction of a Mithraic shrine. Mithras was the favourite god of the Roman soldier; the cult made much of the symbolism of fire, and fire was said to appear super-naturally upon the altar. The god was a hero of whom notable feats were reported, and the religion appealed power-fully to strong men. Women appear to have little or no place among its devotees. Historians tell us that there was a time when Mithraism was so successful a rival to Christianity that, humanly speaking, it had an excellent chance of be-coming the dominant faith throughout the Roman Empire. Two things impress anyone who examines this shrine, a replica of one which had been resorted to by the Roman legions stationed along the Rhine. First, behind the altar it is possible to see the pipe through which the supposedly miraculous fire had been introduced by the priests; the trick was explained. The other, and deeper, impression is made by the smallness of the shrine. Perhaps fifteen people could be accommodated within it; certainly there was nothing sug-gestive of the assembling of a large congregation. A handful of people might watch the performance of a mystic rite, but no provision is apparent for the instruction of the faithful by preaching or teaching, nor could there have been anything of that fellowship of a company of believers which is an integral part of Christian worship. Mithraism demanded the priest but could dispense with the preacher.

When did the preacher become essential to religion ? He appears in Judaism just before the rise of Christianity, for the worship of the synagogue included preaching such as is recorded in the story of our Lord in the synagogue in Nazareth —preaching, that is to say, at that time and place in the service, though the sermon on that notable day was obviously far different from the usual discourse ! This was preaching by laymen, we should notice; the Jewish priest monopolised the sacrificial function, but the task of explaining and teaching the faith was never vested in him exclusively; every parent had the honour and responsibility of teaching the generation to come about the facts of the faith. With the advent of Christianity, however, preaching developed on a larger scale. It was an age of propaganda, and exponents of the new Oriental religions advocated their creed at street-corners and in hired lecture-rooms; it seems, though, that in these religions the ritual bulked more largely than the teaching.

What amount of preaching is there in the non-Christian religions of our own time ? It is a question for the experts. Certainly Judaism still possesses the preacher, and apparently he is still, technically, layman and not priest (though, if of the tribe of Levi, he may also be a priest—but he has no altar at which to minister). What about Mohammedanism ? It is often said that all its adherents are missionaries, but does it employ the preaching method, the gathering of congregations at set times for instruction in the faith, and for the winning of converts ? We have the impression that such converts as are gained are won as the result of private conversation, but this may be a mistake. Outside the three monotheistic religions, (Christianity, Judaism and Mohammedanism, which have a historical relation) preaching seems to be rare.

In 1 Cor. i. 21 Paul declares that God resolved to save those who believe " through the foolishness of the pro- clamation "—not " foolish preaching ", yet certainly through the preaching of a message that looked foolish. Now, the resort to preaching implies much that is important ! It is a declaration on God's part that men are able to hear His word and competent to decide upon it. It gives the mind of man its rightful place; on the one hand, it will not unduly exalt the intellect by supposing that it can dispense with a com- munication from without, nor on the other hand will it despise the mind by reducing it to something that must be stunned by impressive ceremonial but cannot be allowed to register a judgment. And when preaching means the gathering *together* of many people, then there is an implicit declaration of the universality of the Christian message. It is thereby shown that the Gospel is no merely private concern, that it is for all types, all times, all temperaments, that it is social in its applications, not merely individualistic. It would be impossible to say that preaching began with Christianity, but it seems true to claim that the great age of preaching started with the coming of our Lord, and the golden ages of our faith are golden times for preaching.

You probably first believed *through* preaching; do you still believe *in* preaching? It must be preaching of the declaratory kind; the " preacher " often mentioned in the Book of Ecclesiastes was probably rather a debater, and whilst debate has its necessary place the pulpit is for proclamation rather than for speculation and enquiry; work of the latter sort should be done beforehand. If you believe in preaching, do you undertake the work? Or, if you feel you lack the call and the gifts, do you support and encourage it, remembering that the congregation makes the preacher? And do you continually pray for the blessing of God on those who are His messengers? If ours is pre-eminently the religion of preaching, we must all co-operate in the glorious task.

VII

ARE THERE TOO MANY PREACHERS?

QUEEN ELIZABETH once declared herself " offended at the number of preachers ", and instructed Archbishop Grindal that " it was good to have few preachers in the Church, and that three or four were sufficient for a county ". The poet who wrote of God's victorious deliverance in Ps. lxviii. thought it impossible for such tidings to be told too often or by too many heralds, and cried: " The Lord gave the word (the announcement of deliverance); those proclaiming it were a great army ! " (The word for " proclaiming " occurs also in Isa. xl. 9, where it might well be rendered, " O Evangelist Zion "). Shall we rejoice with the psalmist or deplore with the queen that the heralds of the Gospel are a multitude ?

Christian preachers were once described as " men that have turned the world upside down ", and the phrase is not exaggerated. Sermons can be lifeless and negligible, admittedly; they can also be " mighty through God to the pulling down of strongholds ". The vast majority of preachers must naturally do their work with little earthly recognition; fame passes them by, but they are content to wait for a nobler verdict than popular applause, and they appeal to Him Who will say of their work and of themselves: " Well done ! " Yet there have been occasions when a sermon was epoch-making. It was like the last note of the trumpet in the final encircling of Jericho; it gathered up into itself all the previous preparation, all the weary and seemingly useless effort, and, as its clarion call rang out, " by faith the walls of Jericho fell down ". Such an event happened on Sunday, 31st May 1792, when William Carey preached at Nottingham on Isa. liv. 2, 3. That sermon may well be regarded as the trumpet-call which summoned forth the great army of modern missionaries ! Yet it was not an outwardly important event. The service was held in a plain white building which would only hold about two hundred people, and we do not know that the place was at all well filled. The occasion was a gathering

3

of the Northampton Baptist Association, and since only seventeen ministers came as representatives it is possible that other delegates would scarcely bring the company up to fifty. Moreover, since the service was held at 10 a.m. it is unlikely that many other hearers would be present. Yet it is well to note that this ten o'clock service had been preceded by a prayer meeting beginning at six in the morning; is part of the explanation of what resulted from the sermon to be found in that preliminary session for prayer, and is the lack of appeal in modern preaching to be found in any disuse of the practice of united prayer by the congregation beforehand ?

Almost everyone knows how the preacher departed from the practice of his day, which divided a sermon into many involved " heads ", with elaborate sub-divisions, and instead gave the two memorable sentences: " Expect great things from God: Attempt great things for God ". S. Pearce Carey (a direct descendant of William Carey and his best-informed biographer) reminds us that Carey had been a shoemaker for seventeen years, " making things in his workshop in pairs. This sermon fell under the unconscious power of the same habit. They certainly are the right and left foot shoes for every pilgrim and soldier of the Kingdom ". How wise Carey was, also, in putting " Expect " before " Attempt " ! And how interesting it is to see that the eighteenth-century missionary (though tent-making was not his trade) found a picture and a message in the structure of the tent, like the great missionary Apostle of the first century !

What happened because of Carey's sermon ? At first, apparently little ! The sermon was commended, the preacher thanked—but he was not content with that ! Next morning his urgent word was spoken, " Is there nothing again going to be done, sir ? " That stirred Fuller to action, and before they separated a further resolution was taken, which at Kettering in October of the same year resulted in the formation of the Baptist Missionary Society.

That is what a sermon, under God's blessing, can achieve ! And can we have too much of such preaching ? We can have too much of sermons which are calmly and coldly uttered and heard without purpose or resolution. Now, suppose we made a covenant, every one of us, preachers and hearers, that when

we next go to the house of God for the ministry of the Word
we will put to ourselves Carey's challenging question: " Is
there nothing going to be done ? " Do you remember that
Peter's hearers on the Day of Pentecost immediately realised
that action was required, and they called out, " Men and
brethren, what shall we do ? " Any business meeting should
be prepared for by the drawing-up of an *Agenda*; it is a
thought-provoking word, for it simply means " things that
must be done ". What would happen if every preacher,
having prepared his sermon and himself, waited prayerfully
whilst he drew up a list of " things that must be done " in
the light of his message, and if every hearer, at the conclusion of the discourse, sat in silence to discover what, on
the basis of the truth just declared, he himself ought to do ?
There would be point and purpose in Christian preaching
which would have immeasurable consequences.

God still gives His word, and those who proclaim it are a
great army ! They include the noble company styled " lay
preachers ". Who would not covet fellowship with and service
to these ambassadors for Christ ? Men upon whom so much
depends will be wise to lay emphasis on knowledge of the
Bible. Carey's devout study of the Bible obviously had
much to do with his felicitous choice of a text for his historic
sermon, and congregations still tend to recall a sermon by
remembering the text. Yet all who deal with preaching must
remember that the preacher is more important than his
preaching, for in preaching it is personality that tells. But
the preacher's personality is affected by the listener's personality, and so we come back again to the joint responsibility
of pulpit and pew for Christian preaching. We have not
really made too much of the sermon ; we have made too much
of it, perhaps, as the eloquence of man, but not enough of
it as the word of God. Let us refuse to regard the sermon
in any lesser light ! And let us expect great things when we
preach, for only so can we attempt great things !

Dr. H. H. Farmer's Warrack Lectures on Preaching (" The
Servant of the Word ") contain the suggestion that the
preacher might well have inscribed over his desk, as a motto
for every sermon, " Behold I stand at the door and *knock* "—
for the sermon ought to have " this summoning note ". And

then he suggests a companion motto: " Please do not knock unless an answer is required " !

Fellow-preachers, knock ! The matter is urgent. Fellow-hearers, " an answer is required ". " Consider what answer I shall return to Him that sent me " (2 Sam. xxiv. 13).

VIII

FORGOTTEN SERMONS

How long do sermons last? Too long, says some hearer—
not himself a preacher! Not long enough!—so thinks some
earnest servant of Christ, burdened with the fewness of his
opportunities, the extent of his message, the limits of his
powers, and the vastness of the issues that depend upon the
preaching of the Word. Edward Irving declared to his
protesting elders: " I am resolved that two and a half hours
I will have the privilege of ". The days of the lengthy sermon
have passed away, and we must make up for the lessened
time by increased passion and urgency both in preaching
and in listening. For listening often makes preaching !

My question, however, is not about the time sermons take
in delivery, but as to their duration in influence. How long
do sermons *live* ? Some of course are still-born, but we are
now concerned with those messages which come from a
believing heart and a convinced mind. How far do they
affect a subsequent day ? In the volume entitled *The
Great Victorians* Lord Ponsonby writes about Gladstone,
and discusses how far oratory contributed to the great states-
man's amazing achievement. On the whole, Lord Ponsonby
is sceptical about the effect of the spoken word, especially the
word from the pulpit: " The influence of the sermon is
notoriously ephemeral. . . . The great preachers of the
past are all forgotten, their sermons are never read, yet in
their day they stood very high in the estimate of their fellows ".
Is this true ? Does it matter ? Yes, it matters greatly, for
Christian life cannot be strong and enduring if Christian
preaching makes but a transient impression. It is not a
question of the preacher's fame, but of the abiding usefulness
of the preacher's labours.

Our estimate of the enduring life of sermons will depend
largely on our attitude to the preacher's message, and I do
not know where Lord Ponsonby stands in this respect. Clearly,
no one will think much of the influence of a sermon if he is

out of sympathy with the faith the sermon proclaims. Gladstone himself, Lord Ponsonby's hero, had the highest con-
ception of the importance of sermons, and missed no opportunity of listening to preachers; Newman, Spurgeon, Keble
and Chalmers (whose sermon took one hour and forty
minutes), were all rewarded by his close, sympathetic and
earnest attention, and a perusal of the numerous references
to preachers and preaching in his biography convinces me
that he regarded the pulpit as a means of grace—and grace
can never be " ephemeral ".

Principal Charles Edwards, of Bala, once said: " A great
preacher is Christ's last resource ". Probably the phrase
needs some correction, yet it hints at truth. Again and again,
in dead periods of the Christian church, some prophet of the
Lord has appeared, and a great awakening has followed.
John the Baptist in the desert of Judaea, Savonarola in
Florence, John Wesley in England, William Booth and his
comrades—these all illustrate that God was pleased by " the
foolishness of the preaching " to save those that believe.

Yes, it may be replied, but who reads old sermons?
" Ministers are soon forgotten ", said Dr. Hamilton of Leeds.
Try to sell to a second-hand bookseller a volume of sermons,
and you will scarcely get a hearing; enquire of him as a
purchaser, however, and he, so loth to buy, will be eager to
sell! It is not only the estimate of the book-market. Most
lamentably, it must be admitted that sometimes certain
preachers have a very slender faith in the " worth-whileness " of
their calling. In 1925 Dr. Hensley Henson held that not only
preaching but all forms of public speaking would be killed
by the competition of the printed page and the wireless.
" Broadcasting will complete the destruction of oratory both
as a fine art and as a powerful agent for shaping men's
thoughts." He also laid the blame for " the decay of the
sermon " upon educational changes, the dominance of music
in services (" The lovers of fine music are rarely also lovers
of good preaching "), the mobility of congregations so that
preachers cannot preach courses of exegetical sermons, but
must depend on a single utterance, and (especially) the decay
of interest in theology. There is much truth in all this, but
it may also be urged that broadcasting has actually increased

the number of sermon-hearers. Preaching, however, will
never seem an important or significant function unless we
regard it as something quite other than the pleasing exercise
of the orator's art. A line from an old hymn refers to one
Biblical phrase thus: " Life from the dead is in that word ".
That should be true of every pulpit utterance. Did we so
listen last Sunday ? Did we so speak or teach ?

" Ephemeral "—lasting but for a day, like the life of a
butterfly ! Perhaps, however, when the sermon is forgotten
by the hearer it may live on in another fashion. We are
influenced by a great many things we have long forgotten,
and memories can be revived, so that chords that were broken
will vibrate once more. Who can tell when a sermon is
" dead " ? When its phrases and its illustrations are no
longer remembered, it survives in the moulding of life by its
teachings. It is not a question of how long its echoes are
heard, but of how long its power lasts. The preacher's true
aim is not that he may be quoted but that his Lord may be
obeyed.

Everyone knows about the Colchester preacher whose
appeal went to the heart of C. H. Spurgeon. That preacher
has not been certainly identified, and it is questionable whether
he ever knew what had been accomplished on that snowy
Sunday morning. Did he think that his work had been
" ephemeral " ? That sermon lived, however, in every one
that Spurgeon preached; it lives now in the sermons by
the great preacher still being sold and read; and it also lives
in all the men and women brought to Christ under that
preaching, and in their converts and in their converts' converts
unto the end of the age. Who can assign a limit to that ?
Every word of faithful witness can claim the spirit of the
ancient word spoken concerning Samuel: " The Lord let
none of his words fall to the ground ".

What has all this to do with those of us who are not, in the
strict sense, preachers ? " Much every way ", as Paul would
say, for we all have to consider whether we are working for
time or for eternity. Who can give his best and utmost to
tasks that have only a trifling and passing worth ? It is
unhappily true that multitudes now earn their bread by
routine duties that serve passing fashions or minister to mere

caprice; what is the significance of lives so spent? Ah, but that is not the whole story! We live unto God; in Pauline language, again, our real life is " hid with Christ in God "; our true service is for Him, and it has lasting worth. Such Christian service as we can render here does not pass away when memory no longer holds a record of it; it is written imperishably in the archives of heaven. " To spread a sounding name abroad " is not our proper business, nor need we consider how much recognition we get here. Though men forget, God remembers, and He is not so unrighteous as to forget our work of faith and our labour of love.

How many sermons have you heard in the course of your life? Confessedly, there are few that we can remember with any close verbal accuracy; others live in memory by scattered phrases and striking similes; far more live because we can still see the preacher and feel the impression of his consecrated personality. What of the rest? We pray that they may live in their hidden influence on life, buried deeper than memory, built into the foundations of faith!

Whenever we next listen or preach, let us pray, that the sermon may thus last!

IX

A PUZZLING PROVERB

PROVERBS are Everyman's wisdom. They are coined by some unknown genius, who has the most unusual gift of seeing life from the ordinary man's point of view and expressing what he sees in clear and memorable phrase. Perhaps proverbs always have more authors than one; their first inventor's work may be altered and improved by others, so that the final result can be credited to no one in particular. Whatever other quality a proverb may have, it should certainly possess that of clearness of meaning. Who would trouble to repeat the unintelligible, and how would " the man in the street " interest himself in it sufficiently to remember it ?

A greater part was probably played by the proverb in Hebrew literature than we sometimes realise. Jer. ix. 23 suggests that " the wise man " is as important as the mighty man or the rich man ; should we modernise unfairly if we styled them philosopher, warrior and capitalist ? However that may be, Matt. xxiii. 34 definitely names " the wise man " as one of the messengers sent by God to the Jewish people. There may well have been a much more extensive literature than the so-called " Wisdom " books which remain (such as Job, Proverbs, Ecclesiastes and—in the Apocrypha—Ecclesiasticus and Wisdom). Rich and hidden treasures are to be found in the Book of Proverbs, but one saying in the book is baffling; the difficulty is caused not so much by the task of finding a meaning as by the multitude of possible meanings.

In Prov. xxiv. 27 (R.V.) we read : " Prepare thy work without and make it ready for thee in the field, and afterwards build thy house ". There is practically no problem of translation here, and on the surface the words may appear plain; what lesson, however, is intended to be taught ? The commentators are not very helpful; they do not seem, as a rule, to have asked themselves what picture the devotee of proverbial wisdom would have before his eyes when he uttered this piece of advice. Sometimes they suggest that what is here commended is method in work; fulfil your tasks in their proper order. Reference is made to the procedure adopted in building the Temple, (1 Kings vi. 7), according to which the house was built of stone " made ready at the quarry, so that there was neither hammer nor axe nor any tool of iron heard in the house, while it was in the building ". Frances Ridley Havergal's verse expresses this:

> " Now, the long and toilsome duty,
>   Stone by stone to carve and bring;
> Afterward, the perfect beauty
>   Of the palace of the King. "

Such an application lifts the proverb from a prosaic bit of prudence to a sublime prophecy. Our present life would thus be regarded as lived " outside ", " in the field ", *i.e.* the harvest-field, but when our work is completed we leave the field for the home. Yet the interpretation needs to be supplemented from the New Testament, for in what sense can *we* build that home ? Then memory recalls the words of the Master we serve : " I go to prepare a place for you ". Whilst we are working " without ", He is preparing the home within.

Other interpreters understand the proverb to be addressed to the type of young man who rushes into matrimony on too slender a salary ! Moffatt accepts this meaning, and becomes romantic in his rendering : " First work your farm and till the soil; then you can marry and set up house ". If we could accept that exegesis, it would be tempting to employ the words as a warning against marriage with furnishing on the instalment system, but that is a modernisation from which one shrinks. It seems like reading back present-day conditions into ancient history. The Hebrew farmer who had a field to cultivate surely possessed sufficient property to justify marriage. Of course, it is true that " to build a house " can have the meaning " to found a family ", but the question is not whether the rendering can be justified but whether it is likely to be the intention of the speaker. In any case, readers of this volume are not in need of any warnings against imprudent wedlock !

Does the proverb mean: " Till your farm before you build your farm-house " ? It has been said that we should try to discover what picture the proverb would bring before the mind. Proverbial sayings are very largely pictorial in character; that is why they maintain their hold on memory. Most people have visual memories, and a good proverb conjures up a scene which impresses the mind more than abstract argument. For years this proverb has recalled the stories read in boyhood about early pioneers in Canada. The settler would take up his holding of prairie land, and set to work to cultivate it, to fence it, to bring it under control. Whilst this hard initial labour was in progress, he and his family were contented with a rough wooden shack, but as conditions improved and life became more settled the rough shack was exchanged for or converted into a comfortable and more durable dwelling. Work came before comfort, the farm before the farm-house. So long as that was necessary and unavoidable, it could be justified, but there are limits to the wisdom of such advice. After all, the farmer lives *on* the farm but *in* the farm-house, and we are learning to-day that dwellings fashion character.

Still one more interpretation is given by the marginal reference to Luke xiv. 28, " Which of you, desiring to build a tower, doth not first sit down and count the cost, whether he have wherewith to complete it ? ". It is not a perfect parallel, though, for our Lord's words counsel calculation, whilst the proverb enjoins labour. However, the two lessons are related.

In the multitude of counsellors there is wisdom, but the multitude of explanations we find confusion—still more, in the number of possible applications. In *The Expository Times* for October, 1942, Professor Gossip recalls a occasion when James Denney heard Spurgeon preach on the text " Return, return, O Shulamite ". Spurgeon confessed he did not know which of two varying interpretations to choose; " accordingly, to make sure that he got at the real intention of the Scripture, he preached with passion from it, first in the one sense and then in the other ". Professor Gossip thinks there is something to be said for this procedure at times. It is certainly a very tempting method for a preacher, yet, as Dr. Austin Phelps said, " The meaning of the text *is* the text. . . . A misapplied text is no part of Scripture ".

When we cannot decide between varying explanations, perhaps it is our duty to put the full facts before the listener, in order that he may decide. Occasionally, however, there are cases where *all* the meanings may be true, in the sense that, in addition to the writer's first intention, the unfolding purpose of God has given the words a deeper and wider application. That was the case with the famous prophecy of Caiaphas, and it may be so with this many-sided proverb. At any rate, here are set forth some possible elucidations and applications, and if we are still puzzled as to which we should select, we may thank God for the embarrassment of the riches of Holy Scripture.

X

A SUSPENSE ACCOUNT

In 1925 Sir Flinders Petrie read a paper in Birmingham in which he pleaded for the necessity of what he called "a suspense account", to contain matters which (in the phrase of the Scottish verdict) are "not proven". No one, he pointed out, could expect to study all debated questions to the bottom; where, however, we could acquaint ourselves with the real facts, we should take ancient records as in general to be accepted with reason, until other material or facts proved inconsistent. Sir Flinders went on to point out that a difference between records, or between a written record and some physical fact, might be due to one or more of six causes. The divergence might arise from (1) our own misunderstanding, (2) some corruption of the text, (3) partial or differing points of view of the same history, (4) the misconception of some later compiler or transmitter, (5) a sheer mistake by the original writer or (6) deliberate intention. The lecturer said he thought we should find very little left over to the last category. Such treatment was equally due, he claimed, to all writings, religious or secular, pagan or Christian. "To all of us there is visible but a glimpse of the vast stretch of knowledge, human and divine, and we can only add to our own domain some small fringe of that illimitable 'suspense account' which stretches out beyond all our imagination."

It would be hard to find a better code of behaviour for the investigator of any ancient narrative. Who can deny that it is a reasonable and perfectly scientific method of procedure? It will be noticed that the order in which the various causes of error are placed is sensibly modest, since the enquirer is first told to doubt himself, and to question the accuracy of his own understanding; only when all other possibilities are exhausted does he come to the sixth suggestion, which attributes the discrepancy to deliberate falsification. Surely that is proper? If we are more inclined to suppose others mistaken than ourselves, we are dominated by a proud self-confidence which goes far to incapacitate us for the discovery of truth. In Tennyson's phrase, Truth " enters in at lowly doors ". If, moreover, we embark upon our study with a lurking suspicion that the original record is false, we are blind to probabilities and deficient in charity. We have assumed the attitude of a detective who suspects everyone till the criminal is discovered ; detective stories usually show that type of " sleuth " to be a complete failure, and in any case ordinary human relationships would be speedily made impossible by such an attitude. Which is the wiser line of action—to treat all men as honest till they prove to be rogues, or to assume the roguery of every man until he compels us to judge him honest ? No man is so easily cheated as he who is ever on the watch lest he should be over-reached. Now, when we turn to the Word of God, we do so not merely to make discoveries of historical import-ance but in order to establish and to strengthen a spiritual fellowship with the One of Whom the documents speak, and is it not likely that an attitude which would be fatal to human friendships will be utterly destructive of that supreme Friend-ship ?

Of the five causes of any supposed error, it is only the last that undermines faith in the original writer's honesty of purpose ; in the nature of the case there is a strong argument against the possibility of deliberate falsification on the part of a New Testament author, for a variety of reasons. What would have been the motive for such invention ? How would the writer gain thereby ? The " deliberate invention " must have taken place very early, for our evidence leads us back to a point not far from the beginnings of Christianity ; at that time, however, the profession of Christianity was a perilous matter. At the period when a Christian forgery could have been profitable it was too late for it to succeed ! The supposed forgery, also, would need to be supported by the destruction or disappearance of all contrary witness ; it is a vast improbability that this should have happened. Finally, there is the argument from the character of the Book and its proved effects. If we believed that the Book which makes saints proceeded from tricksters, we should have to adopt Jean Ingelow's ironic words about them :

" Gracious deceivers, who have lifted us
    Out of the slough where passed our unknown youth;
Beneficent liars, who have gifted us
    With sacred love of truth ! "

One of the fashions which it is to be hoped war has abolished
is that of " de-bunking ". It was an attempt to bring every
hero and heroine down to ordinary human stature, and one
wonders whether the suppressed motive for it may not have
been sheer envy. It might seem to compensate us for our
own puny achievements if the great of the earth could be
shown not to be so wonderful after all ! Lytton Strachey's
Eminent Victorians illustrated that tendency, and it is interesting to find Mr. H. G. Wood, in his book *Christianity
and the Nature of History*, saying that Lytton Strachey
failed in his attempt to portray these great Victorians " because
what meant everything to the subjects of his portraits meant
nothing to the artist ". Similarly, we need to remind ourselves
that our study of the New Testament will always be a failure
if what meant everything to the writers of it means nothing
to us.

Sir Flinders Petrie has the right to speak about methods of
investigation because he has shown himself to be so accurate
and brilliantly successful in searching into the buried past.
We may be permitted to cite him on another question which
sometimes causes perplexity to the student of Scripture.
There are what seem like duplicate narratives, such, for
example, as the story of Abraham's falsehood concerning his
wife, and in the New Testament the account of the Cleansing
of the Temple, which the Synoptic Gospels place at the end
of the Ministry whilst John records it at the commencement.
" Duplicate narratives " is not a quite accurate title, for there
are significant variations in the accounts, but they are so far
parallel that it is not surprising that the question is raised as
to whether we have not really two slightly-varying reports of
one incident. Each case has to be judged on its merits, but
it is illuminating to find Sir Flinders Petrie protesting against
the prejudice " that no kind of event can occur twice, that
each kind of circumstance is unique and bars repetition ".
Our common proverb declares that history repeats itself.
The story of Abraham's twice-told lie gains corroboration

when we observe in our own lives the tendency of sins to recur, and did not our Lord speak of an evil spirit being cast out and returning with sevenfold force ? Moreover, the story of the Cleansing of the Temple as told by John has no word about the determination of the Jewish priests to put Christ to death. Was it not probably the fact that the first cleansing was tolerated by the interested parties, since they thought it but the hasty impetuous act of a reformer who would soon weary ? But when it was repeated they realised that it was His deliberate and settled policy, and they therefore resolved on His death.

Suppose, however, that you are left with an insoluble problem ? Then you must put it in your " suspense account ", which means waiting for the answer and, meantime, resting in the Lord and waiting patiently for Him ! In company statements of accounts there are occasional references to " suspense balances "; this is not wealth lost or squandered, but held temporarily in reserve. And if we exercise a trustful faith, we shall one day find that these " reserved problems " in our suspense account have suddenly become available riches, for ourselves and for the Church of God.

XI

EARLY CALLED

In 1942 the fiftieth anniversary of the death of John Greenleaf Whittier was celebrated, and many grateful people turned again to his pages. They proved to have all their former beauty and truth. Perhaps they are not in the modern fashion, but it is good to read poetry that has music in it and that dedicates itself to the praise of things that are true, lovely, worshipful and of good report.

One poem especially has a message for our time. It is called " Seedtime and Harvest ". No date is assigned to it, but it clearly belongs to the struggle for the emancipation of the slave. Workers for freedom are encouraged with the certainty of harvest, even if the fields where they sow have a wintry aspect. Then, recalling fellow-workers no longer in this life, Whittier says :

> " But life, though falling like our grain,
> Like that revives and springs again;
> And, early called, how blest are they
> Who wait in heaven their harvest-day ! "

How many readers sorrow nowadays for those who are " early called " ! Others, also, who have not entered into personal experience of such grief, desire to bring comfort to the mourners. Does not Whittier's well-chosen phrase contain some healing suggestion ?

" Early called ", you will notice—not " untimely snatched ". It is not the furtive act of a thief, but a message from One Whose voice is heard, and Who speaks with authority. To be " called " is, in Biblical usage, to be summoned to high and honourable service, to be faced with unique opportunity, to be endowed with all necessary powers, to be brought into intimacy with one's Lord, to be recompensed with His presence and approval now and His bountiful reward hereafter. Is any part of the glory of this lost when His servants are called to service in the land where " His servants serve Him, and see

His face, and wear His name on their foreheads? Any altera tion that death can make in the glory of being " called " will only be such as increases its glory and heightens its privilege.

That is all true, it may be objected, in the case of those who were " early called " like Samuel, before they were " early called " from this life. We have consolation in their going from us, because it is a home-going. But what of the others, those who depart without giving any sign of Christian faith, or who even leave in our memories records that suggest the entire absence of such faith? What shall we say concerning them?

Well, we must not buy comfort at the expense of truth, for it will turn out to be false comfort, unreliable consolation. We are shut up to the New Testament for our knowledge of the future life ; about a state of existence which none of us has experienced or can as yet experience we are compelled to depend either on revelation or speculation, and the latter is an unsafe guide. As ambassadors of Christ, Who has given us in the Scriptures both the credentials and the instructions for our embassy, we fail to find in those Scriptures anything that warrants us in promising salvation in the case of those who die finally impenitent. Our message is the positive one, that Christ is the way of salvation, and that now is the day of salvation. The corollary of this is obvious; there cannot be light without shadow, and the intense light will have beyond its radius a dreadful darkness. None of us, however, is called upon to pronounce a verdict concerning those who pass from us without manifesting the faith that saves. We are in ignor-ance about what passes between God and the soul in the last moments of earthly existence—or, indeed, of what has passed in all the preceding years. Trust in " death-bed repentance " has manifest dangers, but cases of such repentance un-doubtedly exist. Our business is to offer the Christian salva-tion, not to compile lists of the self-excluded. Our com-mission as preachers does not include " the larger hope ", but it does include " the largest love ", the divine love which will do the utmost that can be done for man's salvation. To that omnipotent, righteous and eternal divine love we must leave those about whose faith we can know nothing.

With what relief we turn to these young lives we know, who

in the morning of their days were satisfied with God's mercy! Though " early called " from us, how sure we are that their lives are not ended, and that they will " be glad and rejoice " for ever! With John Ruskin, we ask, " Why should we go into mourning for the guests of God?" Whatever our practice may be about mourning, it is for ourselves we mourn. We have lost their fellowship here for a time, but they have gained what is beyond reckoning, a bliss so great that, if we could realise it, we should rejoice for them to have gained it, at whatever cost in loneliness to ourselves! Alexander Smellie, contemplating such cases of the " early called ", thought of the race between the older and the younger man on the first Easter morn, and said, " They have outrun us, not to the sepulchre, but to the Throne!" In the light of that faith, would we wish it otherwise?

But what leaders we have lost! What future missionaries, evangelists, pastors, thinkers, administrators, in the service of Christ! Often we hear the lament that the national life has been impoverished because of the loss of the potential leaders in the last war. It may be so, but how do we know? The good estate of the Church Militant is dear to the Head of the Church, and it may well be that the passing away of these radiant young believers causes many others to be " baptized for the dead ", so that in the final result the number of Christ's servants is actually increased. We recall the passing of an ardent young preacher whose ministry only lasted seven months, yet, years after his death, his witness is a real power ; " he being dead, yet speaketh ", and he speaks with greater power because of his early death.

Emil Ludwig, in his biography of Lincoln, writes with evident admiration of Stonewall Jackson, quoting his words : " My faith teaches me to feel as safe in battle as in bed. God has decided the hour of my death. I do not concern myself about the matter, but I am always ready." Ludwig says that Jackson " clung faster to this anchorage as the years went by, and seems in actual fact to have died with the words on his lips, ' Very good; everything in order !'" Early or late, whenever the call comes, the Christian knows that everything is in order, and assents to the wise and loving will of God by saying, " Amen! Very good "!

The prophet Micah once exclaimed, " My soul desireth the first-ripe fruit " (Mic. vii. 1). Is it legitimate to make that a divine desire ? The God Who claimed first-fruits from Israel has still every right to them, even when He calls them, in our estimation, too early. The fruit is gathered for use and glory elsewhere; these youthful careers continue in greater bliss and service. The owner of a garden may surely gather its flowers in the spring, not only in late summer and autumn. Supposing Christ to be the Gardener, we are sure that He guards what He gathers, and promotes those " early called " to the land " where everlasting spring abides, and never-withering flowers ".

If it be right in the eyes of the Lord, let Him do what seemeth Him good. Everything is in order; very good !

XII

HONOURABLE MENTION

IN 1852 Macaulay talked with his nephew and future biographer, Trevelyan, about his History, the first volumes of which had appeared two years before, and the remaining volumes were then in preparation. "He told us (says Trevelyan) of two letters he had received from America—one from a Mr. Crump, offering him 500 dollars if he could introduce the name of Crump into his History; another from a Young Men's Philosophical Society in New York, beginning ' Possibly our fame has not pinioned the Atlantic. ' " Those earnest young men may well be let off with a smile; we like youth to take itself seriously, and if the seriousness is overdone that is better than the opposite fault. But what are we to say about Mr. Crump ? Is it any use saying anything ? Certainly, for there is a large tribe of him ! Perhaps some of our readers bear the name ? An eccentric but powerful preacher of some forty or fifty years ago once read the story of Joseph's dreams from Gen. xl. ending with verse 23 : " Yet did not the chief butler remember Joseph, but forgat him "—and, added the preacher, " His name isn't always Butler ! " Adapting that story, let us say of this pushful type of man, that his name is not always Crump ! We have the nature, if not the name, whenever there rises in our hearts the wish for notoriety, whenever we tire of obscurity, whenever we long for limelight and applause. Of course, we are not so ingenuous as outspoken Mr. Crump; he at least made no concealment of his longings, and was prepared to pay a high price for the desired advertisement. And here is the irony of the whole situation : he obtained mention, but not honourable mention. Forcing himself into the limelight, his littleness is remorselessly shown up. He tried to buy his way into prominence, and found himself in the pillory. Oblivion would have been kinder to him than such remembrance.

Of course, there is a desire not to be forgotten which is not at all blameworthy, but has its roots in deep human affection.

Who of us would like to think that death would at once obliterate all record of him ? We all thank God that when (in the solemn Biblical phrase) " the place thereof shall know us no more " there will be those who treasure recollections of us and look forward to re-union, and the Christian faith warrants and consecrates such longing and expectation. But poor Crump was seeking a cheaper and more tawdry remembrance than that; he sought fame he had done nothing to earn and now only lives as an instance of ridiculous folly.

Oblivion, we have said, would be kinder than some remembrance; here is an instance. Carlyle, in *The Life and Letters of Oliver Cromwell*, refers to Major-General Crawford, " once a loud-sounding well-known man . . . whose history may sum itself up, practically, in this one fact, that he helped Cromwell and the Earl of Manchester to quarrel; and his character in this other, That he knew Lieutenant-General Cromwell to be a coward ". What a devastating record ! Crawford is apparently the only man who ever so misjudged Cromwell as to call his courage in question, and the misjudgment condemns the man who made it. Crawford is stamped as a fomenter of strife and as one who could not recognise a hero when he saw one ! Would you like that record ?

We expect to find all types of human character mirrored in that literature which is at once most human and most divine, the Bible, and we are not surprised to find the foibles of Macaulay's correspondent, Mr. Crump, illustrated in that brainless fop Absalom. Consider what is revealed of him in the statement of 2 Sam. xviii. 18 : " Now Absalom in his lifetime had taken and reared up for himself the pillar which is in the king's dale; for he said, I have no son to keep my name in remembrance: and he called the pillar after his own name: and it is called ' Absalom's monument ' unto this day ". Here is a man whose life has been visited by sorrow; sons had been born to him but had not survived. Sorrow, however, has not done its gracious work of deepening character and strengthening trust. Instead, the man is left with a sense of defeated vanity; he is afraid he will be forgotten after death. He does not strive to make himself remembered by noble deeds such as history records, nor by kindly ministries, such as are gratefully cherished by those whom he served, and whose prayers of thanksgiving are better than trumpeted fame; instead, he erects the tall pillar, in the hope that travellers passing by may ask one another whom it commemorates, and so his story will be told. For a little while his name will live again in the minds of curious sightseers. The incurable vanity and flippancy of the man could scarcely be more vividly revealed. Mr. Crump was willing to pay 500 dollars for an advertisement, and Absalom went to the expense of a sculptured monument. And he lives in history, not with honourable mention but with a name that is a synonym for pride, treachery and ignominy.

Have you noticed how many people are given honourable mention in the Bible, yet their names are withheld? That is an indirect witness, in my judgment, to the sincerity and reliability of the narrative. Invented stories go into great particularity, and imagine names of people and places, dates and details, in order (in Gilbertian phrase) " to lend an air of verisimilitude to an otherwise bald and unconvincing narrative ". Romanism gives the name Veronica to the woman who is said in legend to have wiped the face of our Lord as He went to His cross, and for her reward found His portrait imprinted on the handkerchief she used; " Veronica " is, of course, a name manufactured from the Latin for " true likeness " (Vera-Iconica); the obvious derivation of the name discredits the story. Then, there are guesses at the names of the two malefactors crucified at the same time as our Lord; they are said to be Zoatham and Camma, or else Joathas and Maggatras. The name of the mother of the Virgin Mary is said to be Anna; what is this careful insertion of names but fanciful embroidery of a record that needs no amplifying? From these embellishments we turn with relief to the sobriety of the Gospels. Recall as an example the account of the anointing at Bethany (Mark xiv. 3-9); fiction would surely have endowed the woman who did that gracious deed with a significant and memorable name, but her Master and ours rewards her far more fittingly. " Wheresoever this gospel shall be preached throughout the whole world, that also which this woman hath done shall be spoken of for a memorial of her ". What honourable mention—not of the doer's name but of her deed !

In competitions " honourable mention " usually means a lower standard of success than the winning of a prize, but in the realm of which we are speaking all depends upon Who makes the mention. To be mentioned by Christ is superlatively honourable ! And we are sure of it !

> " Then will He own our worthless name,
>   Before his Father's face,
>   And in the new Jerusalem
>   Appoint my soul a place."

Who wrote the Fourth Gospel ? Like the other three, it contains no author's name. But inwrought into the work, like a water-mark in a document, is the wonderful phrase " the disciple whom Jesus loved ". I am sure that indicates the writer. He had none of Mr. Crump's hunger for notoriety ; he has no pride in his literary skill, his marvellous insight, his supreme privilege as a companion and follower of the Lord. As far as possible, he suppresses his own personality, desiring that all attention should be focussed on his Lord. Only when some kind of reference to himself is imperative for the sake of witness to the facts does he point to himself, and then he names himself in a way that he shares with all Christ's people—" The disciple (not the only one, of course) whom Jesus loved ". Lacking John's shining gifts, and never having seen as he did Christ manifest in the flesh, we adopt for ourselves his signature, and write ourselves among the disciples whom Jesus loves. What marvellous, ennobling, enriching and supremely honourable mention !

XIII

ANDREW BONAR'S BIBLE

In 1839 a journey was taken by Robert Murray McCheyne, Andrew Bonar and two other Scottish ministers to the Holy Land and to centres of Jewish population in Rumania and Austrian and Prussian Poland. On his return McCheyne preached a sermon on Rom. i. 16, " To the Jew first ", in which he claims that " there is peculiar access to the Jews ". In many places it seemed to him and his travel-companions that the only door of opportunity left open to the Christian missionary was the door of preaching to the Jews. In the light of present conditions, it is strange to read that these missionaries more than a century ago found it easier to reach the Jews than Italian Roman Catholics, Moslems in Egypt and Palestine, Greek Catholics in Bucharest and Protestants in Austria and Prussian Poland.

In the course of this interesting and epoch-making journey Bonar and McCheyne visited Sychar. They describe it as lying in the valley between " Ebal, a gloomy barren hill, and Gerizim, a rocky hill, but garnished with gardens ". They visited the Jewish synagogue, and then sought out the Samaritans; " after taking off our shoes, we were admitted into their synagogue to see the MS. of the Pentateuch, three thousand six hundred years old ". Then Andrew Bonar desired to find the well where our Lord talked with the Samaritan woman; he discovered it, but accidentally dropped his Bible down the well. Two years later, however, Bonar recovered his Bible; Dr. Wilson of Bombay persuaded a young Samaritan to allow himself to be lowered by ropes into the well, and all that still remained of the Bible, after two years in the water, was recovered and ultimately sent to Andrew Bonar. At the jubilee of the Scottish Mission to the Jews in 1889 Bonar displayed the Bible, greatly to the interest of Scottish children, and it was then deposited in the Children's Missionary Museum in John Knox's house, Edinburgh.

The young Samaritan was named Yacoob esh Shellaby,

who later became Sheikh of the Samaritans, and in 1887 visited Great Britain in order to ask for aid for his people; he wrote to Dr. Bonar saying there were then only a hundred and fifty Samaritans, and they were very poor. He recalled the Old Testament command, " If thy brother be waxen poor and fall into decay, then thou shalt relieve him ". Very persuasively also, this Samaritan reminded Bonar that " In your book your Master tells the story of the Good Samaritan that relieved a man that had fallen in among thieves, and He said, ' Go and do likewise ' ". Andrew Bonar was able to secure some funds to relieve Samaritan poverty.

Now, something can be added to the story of Yacoob esh Shellaby. In 1887 Hodder & Stoughton issued two books which contradicted each other on the question as to whether the Samaritans were extinct. Dr. Edmond Stapfer, of Paris, in *Palestine in the Time of Christ*, wrote that " the nineteenth century has witnessed the death of the last of the Samaritans ". Canon Bell, of Cheltenham, published in his *Gleanings from a Tour in the East* the statement that about seventy of the Samaritans still survived. The question was set at rest by the visit to Britain of Yacoob esh Shellaby. He appealed to C. H. Spurgeon for assistance, and received it. He attended a service in the Metropolitan Tabernacle, and afterwards saw Spurgeon in the vestry. Spurgeon describes him thus : " He is a giant among men in size, with a happy, intelligent, generous countenance. He sacrificed a lamb upon Mount Gerizim at the last Passover. . . . He said his people were few. All told, they do not now number two hundred ". An interesting study in the conflict of authorities !

This Eastern visitor gave Spurgeon a portion of the Samaritan Pentateuch and a Prayer-book with Hymns. Here is the letter accompanying the gifts :

31 SOUTHAMPTON STREET, FITZROY SQUARE,
September 6, '87.

DEAR SIR,—With pleasure and very happy I send Prayer and Hymn Book and part of Pentateuch for you to keep them to remember me. If you be so kind enough to know any lady or gentlemen to give me letter introduction

to, thank you very much. I want to return home in short time. Thank you for your kind. I will pray for you between the two mountains.—Believe me, yours sincerely,
                                    YACOOB ESH SHELLABY.

While there are obvious errors in the wording, not a word is misspelt, and the handwriting is remarkably clear. Would that all Britons wrote their native language as legibly as this foreigner !

How interesting it would be if we could trace the further history of this man who recovered a Bible, only part of which appealed to him ! For the Samaritans do not accept any books of the Old Testament except the Pentateuch, and, of course, reject the witness of the New Testament. Still, Yacoob esh Shellaby's reference to the Parable of the Good Samaritan need not indicate merely a diplomatic use of an excellent ground of appeal; it may well reflect knowledge gained from intercourse with Christians. Clearly he knew something of the contents of Bonar's New Testament, but he could not have been an avowed Christian, else he would not have signed himself " Sheikh of the Samaritans ", as he does in the books presented to C. H. Spurgeon. Still, he found in Great Britain generous friends who acted the Good Samaritan's part to these stricken and dwindling people. We can be sure that, as he prayed for them " between the two mountains ", Andrew Bonar and C. H. Spurgeon also prayed for him—and who knows what will be the final result of such praying ?

Visitors to the Samaritan synagogue within recent years were shown ancient rolls—one of which is claimed to have been written three hundred years before Christ, a second one belonging to the time of the Maccabees, and then the oldest of all, which they claim to have been written by the grandson of Aaron—an impossible claim, of course. Authorities differ as to the date to be assigned to the present roll, some placing it as early as the seventh century A.D., others as late as the twelfth. The script employed is older than the square character used in Hebrew Bibles and goes back nearly to Maccabean times. In the main, the Samaritan Pentateuch agrees with the Hebrew; such variations as are found are of minor importance. If we could establish the exact date of the separation of the Samaritans from the Jews, therefore, we should be able to test the critical theory which attributes to Ezra or to his period important additions to the Pentateuch. If the separation took place, as Neh. xiii. 28 suggests, near to the time of Ezra, it is altogether unlikely that the renegade priest would have taken with him and introduced into the worship of the rival temple on Mount Gerizim a recension of the Pentateuch which was a recent innovation on the part of the very people who had expelled him. Any Scripture taken to and adopted by the Samaritans in such circumstances must have been surrounded by the sanctity of long usage and acceptance. The argument brought against this is that Josephus dates the Samaritan schism a century later than the Book of Nehemiah seems to suggest; further, criticism now suggests that Ezra followed Nehemiah, instead of preceding him. Do we not need someone to descend into the dark wells of Samaritan history, and might such an explorer not discover a lost Bible at the bottom ?

Andrew Bonar was too great a lover of the Scriptures to be dependent on a single copy, and he and his fellow-traveller had with them Hebrew and Greek Testaments to supply the place of the Bible dropped into Jacob's Well; moreover, if they had not possessed these or had lacked the knowledge to read them, they would still have possessed the Word of God, because of their continual memorising of the sacred text. " Thy Word have I hid in my heart ", each of them could say. Andrew Bonar's Bible was thus, in reality, not merely the copy rescued from the well, nor any similar volume, but that Word written in memory and wrought into his life. Someone said, " A man owns as much of the Bible as he obeys ". Could you lose your Bible ?

XIV

THE INSERTED NAME

IN Acts xviii. 4 certain manuscripts, few in number but significant in quality, and viewed with respect by textual critics, insert some words of high importance. The complete verse, with the additional words italicised, would read thus: " Paul reasoned in the synagogue every sabbath, *inserting the Name of the Lord Jesus*, and sought to persuade both Jews and Greeks ". The evidence for the new phrase comes from what is known as the Western text, and cannot be lightly dismissed, but, apart from technicalities, does not the variant reading commend itself by its inherent probability? There was no motive for inserting the phrase but for the fact that it so evidently describes what must have happened again and again. Our Lord had warned His people against incongruous insertions, when He told them that they must not put a new patch on an old garment, but there were some additions which were obviously justified, and whenever they found an Old Testament promise they had no hesitation in " inserting the Name of the Lord Jesus ".

This is what happened in the case of the Ethiopian eunuch. The reader has a book before him and has no trouble about translation, no problem about inspiration, but he is reading a story about an unnamed hero. Does the writer speak of himself or about another? Is it autobiography or biography? There is only a vague description (" My Servant ") and a pronoun (" He "); that is not enough for complete understanding. Then Philip " inserted the Name " that explained everything: " The Lord Jesus was despised and rejected of men; the Lord Jesus was wounded for our transgressions. All we (no difficulty about inserting a name there! Mine goes in, so does yours!)—All we like sheep have gone astray, and the Lord laid on the Lord Jesus the iniquity of us all ". The question is not about what was in the prophet's mind as he wrote; scholarship is entitled to discuss that, and it gives many answers. But what we need to know is what the prophecy means for us, and the answer is: Jesus Christ, or nothing. Unless we can insert the Name of the Lord Jesus, it is but a piece of ancient history; the inserted Name, however, illuminates the page.

This was the method of early Christian preaching, and it was the practice of those first believers in Antioch, who were always " inserting the Name " into their conversation. People said, " Why are these folk constantly dragging that Name into their talk ? ". So out of the inserted Name they made a nickname, and " the disciples were called Christians first at Antioch ". We, too, must insert the Name, not only into public preaching, but into daily speech and conduct. To do so is to put the key into the lock, the antidote into the poison, the ray of hope into the otherwise hopeless situation.

The Name thus inserted illuminates—but it also dominates ! It is like running up the flag and taking possession of new territory. That is how we came into possession of the Old Testament; it is not certain that Christians would have possessed it, otherwise. Gentile Christians, who were soon the majority in the Early Church, would be prejudiced against this apparently uncouth Hebrew literature, in a foreign speech and a foreign idiom of thought; even Augustine tells us that when he first read the Scriptures " they seemed to me to be unworthy to be compared with the stateliness of Cicero ". But some believer discovered that in prophecy after prophecy he could insert the Name of his Lord, as Philip had done for the help of the Ethiopian eunuch; then other believers did the same thing, and they said, " If His Name fits the Book so well, it must be His Book—and if it is His, it is ours ! " He explained the Book, He dominated the Book, and His people in His name annexed the Book.

Now, our discipleship means that His Name is inserted into our lives; the only key to the mystery of life is that inserted Name ! But has insertion meant domination, or annexation ? Not as fully as it ought ! And the effective way to insert the Name into other lives is to let it mean complete annexation of my own life by Him Whose Name I bear.

The insertion is never intrusion. Cowper spoke of people who keep God out of much of their lives; they " start at His awful Name and deem the God Who made them an intruder on their joys ". We have to learn how to insert the Name into our pleasures, our business, our politics. Every area of human life must come under Christ's sway and His Name must prevail everywhere. *The Name of Christ can never be spoken out of place;* do you believe that ? We hear it spoken in profanity in the streets; is it out of place there ? No ! The lips that misuse the Name have deepest need of it ! It is spoken irreverently, but never irrelevantly.

No other name can be universally employed. All others have limited application. A much-loved Methodist minister, J. Denholm Brash, had impressed the grace of Christian love on his people, and after his death one of his class-leaders took up 1 Cor. xiii. and read it, inserting Mr. Brash's name instead of " Love ". " Mr. Brash suffered long and was kind; Mr. Brash thought no evil "—and so on. What a glorious tribute ! But you could not carry it through the chapter; you could not say " Mr. Brash never faileth ", but you could say it of Christ. And we can use the present tense; Mr. Brash " was " . . .; Christ " is " ! Insert His Name in place of the abstract term " Love ", and all the truth of the chapter will remain, and you will have St. Paul's portrait of his Lord.

When the wrong name is inserted, we get tragedy ! Isaac Watts in 1706 wrote a poem in praise of Queen Anne, from whose reign he expected great progress. But Queen Anne died with the promises unfulfilled, and in 1721 Watts re-issued his poem, with a note explaining that he had inserted the wrong name; " George, not Anne, was the name of promise ". Had he lived to our day, he would have had to change the name repeatedly, and he would have said that the only Name of dependable promise is that of the Lord Jesus.

Have you noticed the propaganda trick of incessantly repeating a name ? On the wireless it is called " building up " a personality. Continuous mention of the name is supposed to invest it with prestige; thus Germany has known the wearisome " Heil, Hitler ". It is the advertiser's method. It fails, though, unless the repeated name can bear the weight sought to be reposed on it ; and what other name than that of the Lord Jesus can uphold the claims made ? The other names become cheapened and weakened by repetition, but not His ! How raucous the name of Hitler sounds ! How hollow the name of Mussolini! There was a parody on a Christian hymn which read, " How sweet the name of Buddha sounds ! "—but it never succeeded ! It could not be sung, because it lacked truth and was unable to stand the test of life. Yet the disciples of Christ continue to sing, " How sweet the Name of Jesus sounds ! " and they mean it.

Let us insert His Name into our living and preaching, remembering that the Name can be inserted even if it is unspoken. As far as our report of St. Paul's address at Athens goes, he did not name our Lord in the course of it, yet he undoubtedly introduced all that the Name stands for into certain Athenian hearts.

The cost of insertion is often deletion ! Our names may have to be erased that His may be introduced. The writer of the Fourth Gospel might well have written down his own name in a work of such spiritual genius, but he appears to have desired that His Master might have the pre-eminence; in the Gospel, therefore, when a reference to the author was unavoidable, he omitted his own name and inserted that of the Lord Jesus, describing himself only as " the disciple whom Jesus loved ". That is the point to which St. Paul came when he wrote, " It is no longer I that live, but Christ liveth in me ". " Not I, but Christ, be honoured, loved, exalted; Not I, but Christ, be seen and known and heard ! "

Bengali Christians sing these words:

> " Gods and goddesses throng us with promises;
> But they all will guilty fall 'neath their load of sinning;
> Jesus only, none besides, He's the Saviour !
> Jesus only, none besides ! "

Many famous names have " thronged us with promises ", but none of them is the name that can save. To dominate our own hearts and illuminate this darkened world, let us insert the Name of the Lord Jesus !

XV

MORE VARIANT READINGS

DISCUSSION of the inserted phrase in Acts xviii. 4 makes it desirable to go more fully into the question of variant readings in the New Testament. It is a fascinating study, and its interest and profit ought to be shared with others. All readers of the Revised Version are familiar with the existence of variant readings through the marginal references, introduced in the case of very well-supported readings by the phrase, " Many ancient authorities read ", or, where the evidence is less strong, " Some ancient authorities read ". We do not propose to discuss these cases, which are sufficiently well-known, but since the Revised Version of the New Testament appeared in 1881, additional evidence has become available, and more importance is attached to some other evidence than was then the case. These pages are not intended for those who can enter into the many questions which determine the choice of a reading, and if by chance any such experts should read what is here written they are asked to remember that the writer is addressing himself to those who are laymen in such matters. It will be well to say at the outset, though, that from the study of these variations we can gain much assurance as to the substantial correctness of our ordinary versions. If the changed renderings were all incorporated into our New Testament, practically no doctrinal alteration would result. Deliberate " faking " of the text in the interests of this or that heretical school is extremely rare, if indeed it exists at all; such disagreements as we encounter are the result of honest difference of opinion as to what stood in the original. It may be well also to quote the statement of so great an authority as Sir Frederic Kenyon in his last book on the subject: " The interval between the composition of the books of the New Testament and the earliest extant manuscripts of them has been reduced by a hundred years, and we actually have evidence (small but decisive) of the circulation of the Fourth Gospel in the first half of the second century—

5

that is, within about a generation of the earliest date usually assigned to its composition. . . . Those who are attached to the Bible will be glad to find that all the discoveries which have been so plentiful of late years have tended to confirm the authenticity and general integrity of our texts, and to establish them on a firmer basis than ever " (*The Text of the Greek Bible*, pp. 244, 252: Duckworth & Co., 1937).

The variant to which reference was made in the last chapter belongs to a type of text generally, though a little inaccurately called " the Western text "; let us discuss some other readings which have the same or similar support. Here is one which has a special appeal. In Acts xvi. 30, after the statement that the gaoler " brought them (Paul and Silas) out ", important authorities insert the phrase " having first secured the rest (of the prisoners) ". We may claim for this addition, as for that last considered, inherent reasonableness and probability, and if it is accepted it reveals to us an admirable characteristic in the Philippian gaoler. He is no weakling, easily confused and deprived of judgment by an earthquake shock; rather he displays the quality of devotion to duty so that even in an hour when death seems near he remembers that he is in charge of the prisoners, and it is his business to prevent their escape. A vast body of evidence could be accumulated to prove that those whose eyes have been suddenly opened to the spiritual world are the very people who most usefully and reliably do their duty in this present world while they are fervent in spirit, they are not slothful in business (Rom. xii. 11).

Interesting differences appear in the reports of the word of the Penitent Thief (Luke xxiii. 42, 43). First, accepting the usual reading, we may notice some varieties of punctuation. Certain editors put the comma after " to-day ", so that our Lord's answer runs: " I say to thee to-day, (not waiting till the future coming in the Kingdom), thou shalt be with Me in Paradise ". (Some Syriac sources render " Paradise " by " garden of Eden ".) Other authorities punctuate verse 42 so that the word " Jesus " is addressed by the thief to Christ; that is possibly a suggestion that he had heard the Master's name shouted by the mob, and perhaps (remembering that " Jesus " means " Saviour ") had discerned a deeper mockery beneath the taunt, " He, called ' Saviour ', saved others; Himself He could not save ". A longer substitution is made when the ordinary wording of verses 42 and 43 is replaced by this: " And having turned to the Lord he said unto him, Remember me *in the day of thy coming*. Jesus answering said to him, *Courage !* to-day thou shalt be with me in Paradise ". " Thy coming " is not quite the same as " Thy kingdom "; it could at the most only suggest our Lord's return, not the reign which that return inaugurates. It is unlikely that readers will accept the amended phrase here, nor need they do so, but we should follow the Revised Version and read " *in* " not " *into* Thy kingdom ". " In " suggests what is certainly true, that our Lord will return as King, not merely to become King; He will be accompanied by all royal authority and power, " in His glory, and all the angels with Him " (Matt. xxv. 31). His First and His Final Coming are distinguishable by this circumstance; at first He came in order to become King; He will finally come because He *is* King.

When Luke wrote the account of Stephen's ministry in Acts vi. 11, does he say, as our versions narrate, merely that the opponents " suborned men ", or does he write more fully, " Therefore, *not being able to face the truth*, they suborned men " ? The same verb is used in Acts xxvii. 15, of the ship that carried St. Paul; she " was not able to face the wind ". Whether the inserted words are original or not, they give us a graphic picture of what surely must have been the case. The fresh wind of Stephen's argument was blowing in the faces of these men, like the hurricane called Euraquilo (otherwise, Euroclydon); the sailors wisely " gave way " to the tempestuous wind, reefed their sails, and let themselves be driven before it, until they were carried under the lee of a small island and obtained some temporary shelter. Stephen's opponents, however, have no intention of letting the winds of truth carry them forward; they determine to wreck Stephen, lest they themselves be wrecked, and so they purchase the services of professional perjurers. But what a condemnation to be passed on people who believed in " the Lord God of truth " (Ps. xxxi. 5) ! Condemnation of these bygone palterers with truth will not avail us, however, if we are guilty of the same fault.

Only one more example of a variant reading can be given here; it is found in Acts xiv. 2, where we read of the intrigues by which antagonists of the Gospel made the minds of the Gentiles " evil affected against the brethren ". What happened then ? Were they left unhelped, to endure the rage of the oppressors ? No; if the Western text is followed, we are told that " the Lord quickly gave peace ! " That insertion explains the word " therefore " in the next verses: " Long time *therefore* they tarried there, speaking boldly in the Lord, which bare witness unto the word of His grace, granting signs and wonders to be done by their hands ". This persistence in an otherwise hostile environment, and this record of impressive achievement, find their explanation in the God-given peace. " When He giveth quietness, who then can make trouble ? " And He gave it " quickly " ! Is there any other solution for the problems of mankind to-day than a divinely-bestowed peace ? May we have no peace that is not His gift,and may the Lord give peace quickly !

XVI

WHY ARE THERE VARIANT READINGS?

WHENEVER in the public reading of the Scriptures a preacher substitutes a clearer or more accurate expression, he is apt to encounter a certain impatience in some listeners; in particular, a strong and irrational objection has been made to giving even the renderings of the English or the American Revised Versions. This is due to sheer prejudice, combined with considerable ignorance and an unwillingness to have old associations and ideas disturbed. That slothful state is rare, but Christians who are unfamiliar with the problems of textual criticism are not to be blamed if they feel some disquietude when they are informed of the number of variations in the sacred text. It would seem plausible to expect that a revelation of such tremendous importance would be transmitted to us in such complete verbal perfection that not the slightest doubt could exist as to the smallest letter or accent. We have no right, however, to demand that a divine revelation should conform to our ideas; as Bishop Butler put it, " we are in no sort judges by what methods, and in what proportion, it were to be expected that this supernatural light and instruction would be afforded us ". Had it been for our profit that we should possess a Scripture that left no problems to be solved, no enquiries to be pursued, no difficulties for belief to encounter, without doubt such a Scripture would have been provided; the price of it, however, might be perpetual infancy of the mind ! Since God has undoubtedly willed that our moral life should be a struggle and yet should prosper thereby, we ought not to be surprised if there is an element of struggle in our understanding of His revelation. Bishop Westcott said in 1887 (in his book, *Some Lessons of the Revised Version of the New Testament*) : " We might perhaps have wished, in thoughtless haste, that there had been no room for doubt as to the apostolic words or as to their exact meaning. But further reflection will show how greatly we gain by the fact that the record of revelation, even

69

as the revelation itself, comes to us in the way of human life, exercising every power of man, and hallowing the service of his whole nature. The fact, when we face it, is seen to be a part of our religious discipline ". Side by side with that statement may be placed similarly weighty words by Bishop Lightfoot: " It must be our single aim to place the Bible in its integrity before the people of Christ, and, so long as we sincerely follow the truth, we can afford to leave the consequences in God's hands: and I cannot too strongly urge the truism (for truism it is) that the higher value we set on the Bible as being or containing the word of God, the greater (if we are faithful to our trust) will be our care to ascertain the exact expressions of the original by the aid of all the critical resources at our command ".

Two religions exist to-day which have no problems of textual criticism: Islam and Christian Science. Mrs. Eddy's *Science and Health* has no variant readings; it is too new to have them, and it first appeared in the age of printing, but does anyone feel its reliability is in any way heightened by the fixity of its text ? The Koran is reproduced to-day from one single recension made some twenty years after Muhammad's death, all other manuscripts being then destroyed. The result is that the whole scripture of Islam rests upon the testimony of one witness. Variation is avoided, at the cost of weakening the testimony, whereas our Biblical text gives us a lesser uniformity with a multiplicity of evidence. Which is preferable ? And when the nature of the Biblical variations is studied, it will be found that they are not contradictions of fact but (so to speak) variety of tone, accent and vocabulary. No essential fact, no vital doctrine, is in the slightest degree imperilled by the existence of variant readings.

With that assurance, let us gather together a few more examples. In the Acts of the Apostles the Western text sometimes adds picturesque details to the narrative. Peter's escape from prison contains the fuller statement that after coming out from the cell " they descended *the seven steps* " into the street and went onward (Acts xii. 10). This is unlikely to be mere invention and probably enshrines a personal reminiscence. Commentators have often pointed out that the whole incident is full of details which suggest personal acquaintance with the scene: four quaternions of soldiers, two chains, the smiting of Peter on his side, the first and second ward, the iron gate leading into the city; if, as is probable, these details indicate that the story comes from Peter himself, then the reference to " the seven steps " increases the support for such an inference.

In Acts xi. 27, after the word " Antioch ", an addition of considerable importance is made by some authorities: " And there was much gladness. And when we were collected together, one of them named Agabus spake and signified . . ." The word for " gladness " is used elsewhere by Luke, and means " exuberant joy ". The " collecting together " might mean the re-assembling of the Christian preachers after an evangelistic journey in the surrounding districts, similar to the occasion recorded in Luke x. 17, when the Seventy returned " with joy, saying, Lord, even the demons are subject unto us in Thy Name ! " The most significant feature in the altered reading is the word " we "; if we follow the variant reading we have another (and that the first) of the famous " we-passages ". The most probable explanation of these passages is that they refer to the author of Acts, Luke himself, and if so this changed reading, or rather addition, brings Luke first on the scene and in association with Paul at Antioch in Syria, instead of (as the next passage of this kind would suggest) in connection with the Macedonian journey. Instead of supposing, as students of the ordinary text often have done, that Luke was a Macedonian (possibly " the man of Macedonia "), we should infer from the inserted words in Acts xi. 27 that Luke was a native of Syrian Antioch. Here, of course, very much is mere inference, but probable and interesting inference.

An attractive reading is found in Acts xvi. 4: " Passing through the cities with all boldness they were proclaiming and *delivering* to them the Lord Jesus Christ, at the same time also *delivering* to them the commands of the apostles ". Notice the repetition of the word " delivering "; their proclaiming meant " giving " the Lord to the people, not merely describing Him, and the " giving " of the Lord is mentioned before the " giving " of the apostolic commands. Is there a hint that receiving and even obeying injunctions from apostles is unavailing unless at the same time there is a receiving of Christ ?

In Acts i. 14, we have the welcome addition of the words " and children " after " the women "; it is good to find at this early stage that the Church has " the child in the midst ". In Acts iv. 24, after " when they heard it ", certain texts add " and perceived the working of God ". In Acts viii. 24, it is said of Simon Magus that " he ceased not to weep bitterly "; his tears resembled those of Peter; was his repentance as genuine and fruitful ? In Acts xv. 29, after the advice of the gathering called " the Council of Jerusalem " (which, according to some authorities, also included " the multitude "), certain words are added which give the essential condition for satisfactory Christian living: " being led (or influenced) by the Holy Spirit ". Instead of the familiar statement in Acts xviii. 17 that " Gallio cared for none of these things ", there is evidence for the reading, " Then Gallio feigned that he did not see these things ".

Do not these variants bear out the assurance previously given, that none of them touches vital matter ? Interesting and suggestive as they are, they still leave it clear that the Divine revelation is sufficiently intelligible and reliable for each one of us, a way of life in which " the wayfaring man ", that is, the ordinary traveller, need not go astray.

XVII

NEW TESTAMENT TRANSLATIONS

" *Which, being interpreted, is* . . ." The phrase occurs some ten times in the New Testament, and is worthy of greater notice than the casual reader would be likely to give it. For one thing, it serves as a useful reminder of the important fact that our New Testament is related to and vitally linked with the Old Testament, for in most cases this phrase introduces a quotation from the ancient Hebrew scriptures. Forgetfulness of that relationship subtly affects our understanding of the New Testament teachings; for instance, our doctrine of the Atonement is likely to be weakened and *anaemic* (a perfectly fitting adjective !) if we ignore the light thrown upon the sacrifice at Calvary by the Old Testament offerings. Again, when the Old Testament influences upon the Apostle Paul are remembered, we shall read such a reference as 1 Cor. i. 2 (" all them that in every place *call upon* the name of our Lord Jesus Christ ") with the conviction that the Apostle is ascribing deity to our Lord—for " call upon " means " invoke in prayer ", and the Old Testament makes it clear that the monotheistic Jew offered prayer to none save God.

Instances of that sort might be multiplied, but a second reminder is given us by the recurring references to " interpretation " (by which is meant " translation "). They recall us to the obvious, and therefore easily overlooked, fact that though through the divine mercy we read in our own tongue wherein we were born the wonderful works of God, we are dependent upon translators and translations. Though the miracle of inspiration shows itself in the fact that the Scriptures are wondrously translatable, so that the essential message of the Gospel can be spoken and read in every speech current among men, yet there are inevitable differences in meaning when words written in one tongue are reproduced in another. Let it be made clear that the differences are secondary; thank God there is no monopoly of the truths of the Christian redemption reserved to the minority who have access to Hebrew and Greek ! Scholarship is an attendant minister within the household of faith, never the porter at the door ! That true Christian scholar, Dr. James Denney, wrote: " Nobody values a classical education more than I do; but the things you can ' howk out of the original ', as Barrie says, are not things which accompany salvation. . . . What a man can't find in King James's version has little to do with the Kingdom of God ". For more than forty years the writer has been a student of the Greek Testament, and his debt to it and delight in it are daily increased, but often as he employs that key to the treasure-house of the Word of God he is reminded of our Lord's words concerning some who possessed " the key of knowledge " and never used it; they did not admit themselves, and others they locked out ! (Luke xi. 52).

The translator can act the part of Phurah, aiding others to see what would be hidden save for his guidance. How great is our debt to men like Wiclif, Tyndale and Cranmer ! Sometimes they seize upon slight turns of expression which later translators miss. Wiclif, for instance, renders Acts iii. 26 thus: " God raised His Son first to you and *sent Him blessing* you " (spelling modernised). Now, that is different from the usual rendering: " Sent him to bless you ", which suggests that blessing was the object, the purpose of His coming, whereas Wiclif, following the Greek accurately, saw that blessing is the actual result of our Saviour's advent. The difference is important, for a purpose might not be realised, whereas the result is achieved, not merely hoped for, and present, not merely future. Between Wiclif, in 1380, and Dean Alford, in 1849, no translator known to me preserved this shade of meaning; Adolf Schlatter did so in his modern German version published in 1931. It ought to be said that the usual rendering is justified by the argument that the present tense is used here (as is often the case) with a future meaning, but it may well be claimed that the future meaning should only be given where the present participle cannot have its ordinary sense, and that is not the case here.

In 1881, as we all know, the Revised Version of the New Testament appeared. It was calamitous that many loyal Evangelicals gave the Revised Version so cold a welcome. It had blemishes and faults, undoubtedly, but it was a more accurate rendering based on a greatly improved text, and though long association had endeared the Authorised Version to countless readers it would have been better if those who cared more than others for the Word of God had been more open-hearted and open-minded towards this more faithful representation of it. Against the Revised Version it was truthfully charged that it sometimes sinned against literary taste; one of its greatest lapses was rightly criticised by Sir Edward Clarke, who pronounced the translation of Rev. xxi. 23 (" the lamp thereof is the Lamb ") to be " an intolerable jingle ". The attention of readers of the Revised Version may be drawn to the American Revision, of which comparatively little use is made in this country. We wish our Revisers had followed the American example and rendered " Holy Ghost " uniformly by " Holy Spirit " and had omitted the name of Paul as author of the Letter to Hebrews, for the MSS. the Revisers were following certainly did not justify its insertion.

One significant difference between the British and the American Revisers was that the latter wished to remove some archaic forms of speech to which our own countrymen clung. For instance, " who " or " that " was to be substituted for " which " when persons were intended, and " wot " and " wist " were to be replaced by " knew " and " know ". The Americans were not thorough-going in their practice, however; they still retained such verb forms as " cometh ", " saith " and the like. Both companies of Revisers felt that something of Elizabethan English should still be retained. Were they right ? Probably. Associations of a valuable and powerful sort have gathered round these forms of speech, so that their employment serves as a call to the worshipful mood and a check upon the thoughtlessness which may lead to irreverence. We can test the matter for ourselves if we study the effect produced on our minds by the use of " You " for " Thou " when God is invoked in prayer. Now, it would be unwarrantable presumption for anyone to criticise another for such a usage. " Prayer is the simplest form of speech that infant lips can try "; then let the children of the Father approach Him with that form of speech which is natural and sincere in their own case. Nevertheless, when we are considering audible public prayer in its relation to the listening praying company, experience suggests that the use of the modern forms produces, at least momentarily, " a stop in the mind ", so that it is unlikely that such forms will become customary in united supplication. We hasten to say that we are not presuming to dictate to any suppliant the language of his petition; we are only discussing what would be most likely to help others who were joining in prayer under the leadership of another believer.

Now, all this is relevant to the question of New Testament translations, for all the versions which have appeared in Great Britain since 1881 have, we believe, been versions in modern speech; some have been colloquial to the verge almost of vulgarism, but none has kept the stately Elizabethan forms. And it is noteworthy that congregations as a rule do not greatly enjoy the use of the modern versions in public worship, though they may make continual use of them in private. That is an important fact, whatever conclusions we draw from it.

Let us note another significant fact about modern versions. They are in every case the work of a single translator. The Authorised Version and the Revised Version were produced by companies, and Tyndale had helpers, but Moffatt, Weymouth, Torrey, Way, Wade and the others issued their renderings as the result of their own indefatigable but solitary labours. That means that such renderings will be, in a peculiar sense, liable to " the personal factor ", and their authority is narrowed to that of a single mind. Doubtless there were advantages in such limitation of responsibility, and it was in some cases unavoidable, but inevitably there are realms where team-work is preferable.

XVIII

FURTHER TRANSLATION HINTS

WE are not suggesting alterations in printed versions of the
New Testament, but proposing that, in our private reading,
we should occasionally substitute in our own minds a fresh
equivalent for a word or phrase which may have lost its sharp
edge through familiarity, or have ceased through changes of
language to convey its true meaning, or which may even be
an inaccurate rendering. Changes in the printed text should
only be made after long consideration and after consultation
with other competent judges. Here we make personal suggestions—and they are only suggestions. Our aim will have
been achieved even if readers, after consideration, reject them,
for thought will have been stimulated upon the matter.

Much can be learnt from the experiences of missionary
translators. They have to find words for the original Greek
which are more than mere dictionary-equivalents, and knowledge of native customs may render an otherwise suitable
word inappropriate or unfitting. Holman Bentley, of the
Baptist Missionary Society, toiled to provide a New Testament for Congo people, and has left on record some of his
problems. For instance, a word which seemed likely to render
the meaning " holiness " was found on closer investigation
to mean " alms ". Now, if that mistake had not been discovered, it is possible that the native mind might have been
indoctrinated with the thought that alms-giving was related
to holiness, and the old Pharisaic fallacy might have spread
to Congo. When Bentley and his colleagues had to translate
the word " Church ", meaning a body of believers, they first
thought of a word that meant " crowd " or " mob ", but the
Church is more than a mob ! They were guided—surely by
the Spirit of God—to adopt a word which signifies " The
retinue of a Chief ". Is not that a true and beautiful picture-
word ? " The Chief " is the chiefest among ten thousand, the
altogether lovely. And His retinue is composed of those who
follow, who obey, who owe their status entirely to Him. How

proud men are to form part of the Household of King George !
That eagerly-sought distinction is less than we possess
when we become members of the Church of the Lord
Jesus Christ ! Furthermore, the retinue of a chief will include
people with various gifts and offices, but they find their unity
in their common service of their ruler, and apart from him
they are just a mob, a crowd. Has the Church any meaning
or worth apart from her Lord ? He is the Leader, He is
Chief—and when He next calls us to some task or sacrifice,
let us remember that His " Follow Me ! " is an invitation to
join the retinue of One Who is Chief, King of Kings and
Lord of Lords.

Dr. Holman Bentley was advised in his translation work
by Dr. Joseph Angus, one of the company responsible for the
Revised Version, who warned him that the chief difficulty
would be in " preserving the ambiguity of the original ".
Now, there is a fact to be remembered; *the original is sometimes ambiguous*. We are not thinking of a complete uncertainty as to any meaning, but rather of cases where the
original word is so rich in its connotation that it may have
many translations, all justified, all instructive and valuable.
The translator is often compelled to choose one only of a
number of possible, and justifiable, renderings, knowing all
the time that he has only indicated a fragment of the wealth
of suggestion in the original. Here is an instance, taken from
the highly-significant prologue to the Gospel according to
Luke. There the evangelist tells us that his many predecessors
had attempted to narrate " things which are most surely
believed among us " (Luke i. 1). That is the rendering of
the Authorised Version, but the Revised Version rendering
is : " matters which have been fulfilled (margin : fully established) among us ". Each rendering is correct, and yet " the
half has not been told ". G. W. Wade (in " The Documents
of the New Testament ") prefers to translate the phrase thus :
" events that have come to a climax ". We need not regard
these as rival renderings, but rather as each contributing a
further shade of meaning. The root idea of the word is " to
bring in full measure "; it can mean " to fulfil " a task (cf.
2 Tim. iv. 5, " fulfil your ministry "), or " to fulfil " the proof
of anything (so in Rom. iv. 21, Abraham is said to have

been " fully convinced " that God was able to do what He promised). What does it mean in Col. iv. 12, where Epaphras is recorded to have striven that the Colossians might stand perfect and " fully assured (A.V. complete) " in all the will of God ? Well, a scrap of papyrus was discovered in Egypt on which the word occurs in the meaning of a debt that is fully satisfied: " it happens that I have been satisfied in respect of the sums due to me "—that is, no further claim could be made, the full demand had been satisfied. Does the Colossian reference mean that the Christians in Colosse had come to see that every demand they could make on the Divine will had been met—the demand for explanation, for protection, for complete provision ? Not—let us notice— every demand that the inquisitive and assertive human reason thinks itself at liberty to put forward, but only rightful demands. God's will has done by you and me all that can justly be demanded; it has satisfied all the claims we can make upon it; are we " fully satisfied ", in the ordinary sense, with it ?

This has been a digression to show the wide range of the word, and we must come back to Luke i. 1. Combine all the meanings as you read; think of the great narrative which the Gospel according to Luke contains as something that is most surely believed, fulfilled, fully established and brought to a climax. Indeed, the renderings mutually imply each other, for what is fully established can be most surely believed, and brought to a climax. We may each say to another, as Paul said to Timothy: " Bring your ministry to a climax ". And he who commits himself unto his Lord will be able to apply to himself Paul's further words later on in the same chapter (2 Tim. iv. 17), " The Lord stood by me and strengthened me that through me the proclamation (of the Gospel) might be brought to a climax (or fully established, or most surely believed) ". In any case, this word is rich in meaning, and to study it is like discovering " treasure hidden in a field ". It would be a loss if we forgot " the ambiguity of the original " and restricted ourselves to part only of the significance of Scriptural language.

Not all changes in translation are improvements, and some-times the translator, in his search after freshness, introduces an innovation that is unnecessary. For instance, the majestic statement that " God saw all that He had made, and, behold, it was very good " was reduced to bathos by one reviser who substituted the pompous phrase: " He was fully satisfied with all his work ". Gen. xxv. 8 reads " And Abraham gave up the ghost, and died in a good old age, an old man, and full of years, and was gathered to his people ". This was " improved " into the following:' " He died after a long life, having spent his declining years in happiness before he joined the great majority ". That descends from the sublime to the prosaic ! In justice to the author of these two atrocities, let us quote his rendering of the great statement that Enoch walked with God: " Enoch was a constant companion of God ". That does not make the matter any clearer; it was amply clear before; it does make it graphic, however, and one reader is grateful that when he came to that version he had to stop and think, instead of racing on over a page of the Bible he thought he knew quite well.

There is one word, let us remind ourselves, which repeatedly occurs in the New Testament, but for which no full and adequate equivalent has ever been found; it is the word " Grace ". It is an oceanic word, " a vast, unfathomable sea, where all our thoughts are drowned ". What a relief to come to a word that stretches beyond all definitions ! Samuel Davies, successor to Jonathan Edwards, called it " this strange, this wondrous grace, this matchless miracle of love ". It is too great for any dictionary—but not too lofty to stoop to our necessity, and God translates His grace into the exact answer to our problem, so that we find grace to help us in time of need.

XIX

STILL FURTHER TRANSLATION HINTS

ARE there any advantages in not knowing English ? We had better be careful, or else our patriotism may be suspected ! What we have in mind is that there are occasions when a foreign rendering of a well-known word brings out something we had failed to convey by the familiar English word. Perhaps the best thing to do is to be a Briton and a missionary, for then we gain advantages in both directions. Missionaries deserve to have every possible recompense ! Recently it was reported that in colloquial Chinese they say, " The Lord is my refugee-camp ! " What a picture of a word, and how it illustrates the timeless quality of the Scriptures, so that they are, in a true sense the most up-to-date writings in the world ! In some parts of China (so we are given to understand) the Holy Spirit has been called " The One Who brings us round the corner ". Often it is when we turn round the corner that we feel the full force of the tempest; the shock is sudden, the resistance is great. It is then that we need additional help, and we find it in the Comforter, the One Who brings us round the corner.

A Gaelic-speaking friend insists that Gaelic is the most perfect language for conveying Gospel ideas. He gives the following illustrations. (We omit the Gaelic words, lest we should misspell them and incur wrath). Gaelic uses for " contentment " a word meaning " Love mingled with quietness ". For the Gospel the word employed is " The story of peace (or light) ". " Mercy " is expressed by a term denoting " Love going out towards wretchedness ". Suggestively enough, Gaelic speaks of an " excuse " as being " half a statement, or story ". That brings an excuse almost within the category of " a lie which is half a truth—a harder matter to fight ".

What lies beneath the word our versions render " discreetly " in Mark xii. 34. The scribe who was not far from the kingdom of God was seen by Jesus to have answered *discreetly.* That word to-day has a flavour of crafty diplomacy about it, and suggests the wary reply of one anxious not to commit himself too fully. But it is our Lord Who is said to have discerned the discretion of the reply, hence this is His judgment upon it, and He would scarcely have approved of any timid prudence; the word must have a meaning not conveyed by our present word. The Greek word is only employed here in the whole New Testament; it occurs in classic Greek with the meaning " wisely, sensibly ". These meanings are sufficient in most cases, but do they satisfy in Mark xii. 34 ? The Greek word is a compound of the two words for " having " and " mind "; we therefore suggest that the sense here is that the scribe answered " as one having a mind of his own ". That is exactly the quality his answer reveals; he is not content merely to cite Scripture, but he considers it; he possessed not only a memory for the Word of God, but a judgment on its application, and on the relative importance of love for God and man as compared with " all whole burnt offerings and sacrifices ". A man with a mind of his own, which he exercises upon the revealed truth of God, a man with a sense of proportion who puts first things first— no wonder that our Lord said he was not far from the kingdom of God ! Protestantism has always recognised the value and necessity of having a mind of one's own, whilst Romanism has required and cultivated an attitude of docile submission. For example, Newman refers to Jerome, who was a bad-tempered and ill-mannered man, who, when he was opposed, used violent and scurrilous language, a man of pronounced ambition and self-consciousness, whose shortcomings are fortunately overshadowed by his services as a scholar and translator. Now, Newman shows his awareness of the faults mentioned, by saying: " Were he not a saint, there are words and ideas in his writings from which I should shrink; but as he *is* a saint, I shrink with greater reason from putting myself in opposition, even in minor matters and points of detail, to one who has the infallibility of the Church pledged to his saintly perfection ". That is an instance of an enslaved judgment, and for Newman submission to Rome meant that he ceased, on vital matters, to have a mind of his own.

What meaning do you give to the word " kingdom " ?

It has two possible applications, according as we think of the king's rule or the king's realm. The first means authority exercised, the second means the people or the land over which it is exercised. In the United States of America our King has no territory over which he reigns, save the area occupied by the British Embassy in Washington, but wherever there are British subjects in the United States he exercises rule over them; they can be called upon to register for national servive, and they can avail themselves of the fact that he is their king by appealing to the British Ambassador for help in case of need. King Haakon controlled no territory in Norway during the war, but though he did not control the realm his rule was established in the hearts of his people, and because the people acknowledged and loved his rule he was at last restored to his realm. Now, let us apply this distinction to the Bible. Recent scholarship is insisting that in the New Testament the *first* idea of " kingdom " is rule, kingship; of course, the other idea comes in; when God's kingly rule is accepted in anyone's soul, its influence spreads over his life; as the rule deepens, the realm widens. Then it spreads to other lives, and these others, who have submitted to the rule of their King, realise that His will for them is fellowship, so they are gathered into a Church. The Divine kingship results in the Divine kingdom; it would be foolish to emphasise either meaning so that the other is forgotten, but it is all-important to realise which is first. If we think most of what may be called the " extensive " idea of the Kingdom of God, we may be led into the error of identifying it with social progress, and of supposing that the Kingdom is brought into being mainly by our own efforts. One agreed result in recent discussions is that the Kingdom is a supernatural gift, not a human achievement. We are told to pray for the coming of the Kingdom (and of course every sincere prayer commits us to activity); still, what we pray for we believe will come from God, not be set up by our toil. The Kingdom of God is worth searching for like a pearl of great price or treasure hid in the field, but the pearl was not created by the sacrifices the merchant made to acquire it, nor was the treasure amassed by the man who discovered it. These two aspects of the Kingdom might perhaps be sometimes distinguished as present and future; God's rule is a present reality (" Thine *is* the kingdom ") and a future triumph (" Thy kingdom come "). It would never do to separate the two meanings; they are linked as present and future are linked. But would it not be worth while, the next time you come to the word " kingdom " in your Bible reading, to stop and ask whether the word in that context means the Divine rule or the Divine realm, the kingship or the royal domain ?

In 1 Cor. xv. 34 (R.V.) Paul says, " Some have no knowledge of God : I speak this to move you to shame ". A commentator from whom much can usually be learnt interprets " some " as " some *of you* "; does he not miss the point ? Unsatisfactory as the Corinthian Church was, would Paul have denied to any of its members the knowledge of God ? Is he not rather referring to the outsider, who is ignorant of God ? The commentator based his understanding of the verse on the statement that Paul is endeavouring to move his readers to shame, but that seems to justify our interpretation ; the fact that there are people outside our Churches who have no knowledge of God is a matter which ought to cause us shame. Now, we have been speaking of a deeper knowledge of the Scriptures—a most important matter—but what of the knowledge of God, " in the knowledge of Whom standeth eternal life " ? And what of the people who lack it ? Shall not the thought of them move us, who are Bible students, and who " give attention to reading ", to " do the work of an evangelist " ? Thus we shall be moved, not only to shame, but to service.

XX

EVERY MAN HIS OWN TRANSLATOR !

CONSPICUOUS among recent translations is Dr. C. C. Torrey's *The Four Gospels*, based upon the view that our four Gospels were each originally written in Aramaic, and that some obscurities and difficulties in the present Greek text can be explained by supposing that the original Aramaic was misunderstood by the Greek translator. This could easily happen, since Aramaic was written entirely in consonants, the vowels being mentally supplied by the reader. If you have had experience of the use of unvocalised shorthand, you will know that it is easy to mistake the outline of (say) " bad " for such totally dissimilar words as " bed ", " bid ", " bade " and so forth. The context would be a sufficient guide for us to distinguish between the first two words, but the latter pair might easily be confused. If, then, the wrong vowels were supplied, a great change of meaning might result. One most interesting suggestion made by Dr. Torrey is that in Matt. xxvi. 6 instead of " Simon the leper " we should read " Simon the jar-merchant ". " The same consonants would stand " (Dr. Torrey tells us) for either word. Was the alabaster vase bought from Simon ? It is an attractive possibility, but cannot be completely proved. Dr. Torrey thinks that our Lord's command known to us in the form " Take up thy cross " should be " Take up thy yoke ". The yoke would be a wooden beam with a cross-bar, and the word may have had both meanings. Of more importance to us than these varied renderings is the fact that Dr. Torrey's belief that the four Gospels were composed in Aramaic (and, he holds, in Palestine) would imply an early date for their composition. It has been usual to suppose that the Fourth Gospel was written in Asia Minor at a date much later than the other three, but this theory would justify the claim for a much earlier date for it, and our belief in its apostolic authorship would receive additional support.

It would be delightful to linger among the translations,

gaining from each its special contribution, but, with due acknowledgment of our debt to them all, we would make the claim that every man may, in a certain sense, be his own translator. It is not meant that we are all competent to puzzle out Greek, but there is a species of translation of which we are all capable, and which can add immensely to the force of the original. It is the kind of translation which a gifted reader brings to a passage of poetry when he reads it with deep feeling, complete understanding and entire self-identification. Most of us have greatly benefited by the reading of the Bible in public worship when the reader has, by the tones of his voice, by varying emphasis, by due pauses, interpreted that which he read. He translates for our *ears* and, through our ears, for our minds.

Now, much of the New Testament literature was written for people who could not read, but were dependent on some better-instructed brother. In Rev. i. 3 there is a beatitude for both the reader and the listener in the Christian assembly; the office of " reader " was long continued in the Christian Church. The inflections of the reader's voice would supply to the ears of the hearers what is given to our eyes in a modern book by such devices of the printer as the note of exclamation, the question-mark, inverted commas, by the breaking up of the text into paragraphs, and so forth. Can we add these for ourselves as, publicly or privately, we read the Word of God, and thus become " every man his own translator " ?

For instance, how do you pronounce the word " Lo ! " ? It is a very common word; there are more than two hundred instances of its use in the New Testament. The word has surprise, excitement, amazement in it, and its frequent employment indicates to us that the New Testament is an exciting book ! Whenever you come across " Lo ! " do not merely repeat it in a dull, flat manner, but impart to it some accent of the extraordinary, some indication that we are dealing with that which departs from routine. Dare we, to illustrate our meaning, take liberties with the printer's type and the sacred text, and thus render Rev. i. 18 ?—" I became dead, and—look ! *look!* LOOK ! I am *living* for ever ! " The thrill of it ! Translate it into your reading, and let the joy of it throb in your life.

If every man is to be his own translator, are we not entitled to insert some capital letters where at present they do not appear ? Not all will agree with our suggestions, but they may provoke better ones. Put a capital letter with the word " supply " in Eph. iv. 16 : " through every joint (connecting with) the Supply ". In 2 Cor. ix. 10 God is called " the Supplier " ; why may not " the Supply " be a divine title in Eph. iv. 16 ? Another place to be similarly treated is Jas. ii. 1, where " the Glory " is, I believe, to be read in apposition with " our Lord Jesus Christ ". In the Johannine Epistles our versions tamely print " truth " as an abstract noun, but are there not several instances where John refers to that Divine Person Who said of Himself " I am the Truth " ? In 3 John 12, we are told that Demetrius has the witness of all men ; is it not likely that the witness next mentioned should be equally a personal witness ? If so, we should read " and of the Truth Himself ". For what was Simeon waiting, according to Luke ii. 25 ? For what ?—nay, surely, for *Whom ?* For " the Consolation of Israel ". Is not that a gracious and fitting title for our Master ?

Most of us substitute modern terms for phrases which were correct usage in seventeenth century English, but are no longer acceptable. Here are some other substitutions we might well make. For " brethren " read " fellow-believers " ; for " saints ", " God's hallowed people " (but the emphasis is rather on their belonging to God than their being hallowed by Him) ; for " in Christ ", read " in union with Christ " ; for " apostles " we might often put " missionaries ". This is a list that might be almost indefinitely lengthened. We once heard a preacher say " gibbet " for " cross " ; we should not like that change made permanent, but on that occasion it was helpful translation. On the other hand, a modern writer translates " scribes " as " theologians ", and that is not so welcome an alteration (though it starts questions in the mind !)

In an earlier chapter reference was made to the need for breaking up the long interwoven paragraphs of the New Testament into shorter sentences. St. Paul's style especially calls for this. Have you never felt the difficulty of following in the English version the long chain of ideas in that rich and profound first chapter of the letter to the Ephesians ? The

Revisers break up the twenty-three verses into three paragraphs, but even these are too involved for complete and immediate apprehension. Yet Paul clearly expected that his correspondents (among whom were " not many wise ") would be able to follow his linked arguments, his accumulated and related epithets. The reader's voice doubtless helped, as he paused here and there to enable his fellow-believers to follow, but they had another Helper, as we have—the Holy Spirit !

We have come to the secret here ! This is how every man may be his own translator ! That Holy Spirit through Whose ministry the words were written still dwells in the heart of the believer to interpret the Scriptures. He is the gift of the Risen Christ to every one of His people. Reginald Heber was wrong for once, when he wrote:

> " A glorious band, *the chosen few,*
> On whom the Spirit came ".

The record is clear that the whole company, not merely " the chosen few ", the Apostles, received the gift. From another standpoint the same truth of the universality of the Divine bestowal is expressed in Eph. iv. 7: " But unto each one of us was the grace given, according to the measure of the gift of Christ ". When next we read the Bible, let us seek the assistance of the Holy Spirit that we may rightly translate.

Then comes the yet harder task of translating into life and witness the truths made vivid to the mind and precious to the heart ; thus we become " an epistle of Christ, written . . . with the Spirit of the living God " (2 Cor. iii. 3).

To such a translator the Word of God is no mere piece of literature, but the message of God within the soul. Its general promises have personal application. When such a reader comes to the great text, " He loved *me* and gave Himself for *me* ", he will identify himself with the words, agreeing with Luther's statement that " the effect altogether consisteth in the well-applying of the pronouns, wherein there is ever some vehemency and power ". May God make us readers and speakers of the truth of God who experience its vehemency and power !

XXI

TESTIMONY

The Long Week-End is an interesting book by Robert
Graves and Alan Hodge which gives the social history of our
country in the " week-end break " between the two wars.
The period covered, 1918–1939, is well within the memory
of very many people, yet the authors find that the materials
on which they have had to rely—memoirs and contemporary
newspapers—are far from trustworthy; they say, " We have
been recently interested to find widespread disagreement in
the Press about even so recent and important an event as the
German re-occupation of the Rhineland; quite a large body
of opinion is under the impression that it took place in March,
1934, not 1936. We cannot explain this ".

That is a story with many lines of suggestion in it. We
believe the correct year for the event in question is 1936, but
supposing it were 1934, that is only nine years ago, yet uncertainty has already gathered over the matter. Of course,
it would be possible to establish the exact date if access could
be had to our Foreign Office records or German sources, so
that it is not a case of decisive evidence having entirely
perished; nevertheless, on a matter of world-wide importance,
the story of which was flashed round the globe and com-
mented on in well-nigh every country, a matter which every
Foreign Office throughout the world must have investigated,
uncertainty arises within a few years. What amount of
reliability attaches to human testimony, and how far can we
depend on historical evidence ?

Supposing anyone were to cite this instance to you, and to
argue therefrom that our uncertainties must be much more
serious when we are dealing with happenings as distant from
us as the Old Testament events, what would you say ? It is
the sort of question that has been asked, and any of us may
encounter it.

The right plan would seem to be to admit with the utmost
frankness the possibility that there are elements in any

historical tradition which must ever be open to doubt as to details. For instance, it has been stated that historians are unable to determine on what day Charles I. raised his standard at Nottingham. August 22nd, 1642, is usually given, but evidence well worthy of consideration suggests another, though very near, date. To what does this difference amount, however ? What is actually left doubtful because of conflicting testimony ? Our questioner might well be asked to consider the proportion which the uncertain bears to the certain in such cases; he will usually discover that what is in question is small in quantity and negligible in quality. In the instances we have cited, the really important facts are that Hitler *did* re-occupy the Rhineland, in whatever year, and that Charles I. *did* declare war on the Parliament, on whatever day of the year. There is far more certainty than uncertainty in life, far more light than darkness, and this is true of the province of history.

In this argument we are visualising an objector (perhaps it would be better to say, an enquirer) who lacks our trust in the reliability of the Bible, which is based on our own experience and that of the whole Christian Church. To such an enquirer, it might well seem to be a disquieting possibility that past happenings are shrouded in obscurity. Have you a comrade in business or in other realms in such a position ? You cannot cite your faith in order to dispose of his doubt, but it will be legitimate for you first of all to point out (as has just been done) that the area of uncertainty is limited. He might, however, urge that if a comparatively recent occurrence was uncertain as to details, such uncertainty would increase in proportion as more distant history was concerned. That does not necessarily follow, however. Why is there this dubiety about the re-occupation of the Ruhr ? Partly because there has been such a flood of momentous happenings that the mind does not retain the lesser details, and is unable to do so because of the volume of more important things which must be retained. Our modern world, with its newspapers, its telegraph and wireless communications, is more favourably situated than patriarchal times for the spread of *impressions and rumours*, but little (if any) better off for the retention of truth. Quieter ages had time to assimilate and to ponder, and memory was strengthened by use, not weakened by dependence upon records. Distance in time does not therefore of necessity mean a lessened hold upon fact.

Our supposed enquirer ought to be reminded, moreover, that any scepticism about the possibility of accurate knowledge concerning the past will apply to *all* history, not merely to the Biblical narratives. It was no unknown thing in days when the historicity of Abraham was challenged to hear those who questioned it bring forward as irrefutable evidence their own imaginary reconstructions of history. Some of those who have loudly echoed the saying that the Bible should be treated like any other book have been slow to give it the same reasonable and fair treatment as they accord to other literature, and impossible demands have been made upon scripture which the secular historian would never think of making. We have read accounts of primitive man, based on a few relics and much hypothesis, which abound in definite statement and dogmatic assurance, while the authors of such accounts display extreme scepticism about scripture records based on much better evidence. However that may be, he who is sceptical about the possibility of a true tradition surviving from the past has no warrant for limiting his scepticism to the Bible. Some readers will recall a famous book called *Historic Doubts concerning Napoleon Buonaparte* ; it applied the methods of those who regarded the Bible as historically unreliable to the far more recent case of Napoleon, and proved triumphantly that he never existed—a magnificent *reductio ad absurdum*.

Where exactly did that air raid take place ? We have all heard conflicting rumours, but they do not disturb our knowledge that the raid happened, and we appeal finally to our judgment of the reliability of the witness. Having had occasion to depend upon previous statements of his, we accept his testimony now; our act of faith has a good foundation in past experience. We repeat an argument previously used in these pages, and suggest that the Bible stands to us in a position analogous to that of a tried and trusted friend, to whose words we apply the best interpretation, and on whose evidence we can safely rely.

We have all noticed that the Old Testament and the New

Testament alike have a high standard concerning testimony. They are Oriental books, and bribery and threatening have often corrupted Oriental witness, but the Bible insists on witness being corroborated ("That in the mouth of two witnesses or three every word may be established "—Matt. xviii. 16, where our Lord is alluding to Deut. xix. 15 and many similar Old Testament utterances). When our Lord healed the leper, He ordered, " Go, show thyself to the priest " (Mark i. 44); that was an injunction to submit the cure to the test of criticism by the appointed authority (Lev. xiii), however prejudiced and unfriendly he might be. It is the utterance of One Who is scrupulous about truth.

Have you ever asked the reason for the provision in Deut. xvii. 7, that when a man was condemned to death the witnesses against him should take part in the execution? (Compare Acts vii. 58). The reason for it is not just barbaric cruelty, but the deeper feeling that *when anyone has given testimony, he should take the consequences of acting upon it*. The witnesses who stoned Stephen committed themselves in deed to that which they had spoken in words. That is a far-reaching and rightful principle. We who argue in defence of the Bible are witnesses who give a testimony; even if we do not engage in debate, our bearing the Christian name is a testimony; are we acting upon it? Do we commit ourselves in deed to that which our words imply?

XXII

WHAT IT LOOKS LIKE

In his *Confession of an Octogenarian*, Dr. L. P. Jacks recalls an acquaintance of his youth, a veteran soldier who had been wounded at Quatre Bras in 1815. Lady Butler painted a picture of the battle, and a friend took the old warrior to see it. Asked what he thought of it, he replied: " Well, it didn't look like that to me. You see, the lady that painted that picture was looking at the square from the outside where she could see the faces of our men. I was inside, where I couldn't see our own faces, but only the Frenchmen that were coming at us. No sir, it didn't look like that to me ! "

The painter was looking *from the outside ;* that makes a tremendous difference. The point of view determines everything, and there must be many happenings in life which " didn't look like that " to the actual participants. It is worth while to use the illustration to remind ourselves that our judgment of our own and of other times may be wrong because of our standpoint.

The glowing pages of history give us a picture of the events recorded which would probably surprise those who were involved in the great happenings. Were their days so exciting as they now appear to us ? Or were they not, to those who experienced them, ordinary days, uneventful years, with no apparent hint of crisis and no touch of greatness upon them ? We are very sure that the times in which we are now living will be the theme of historians as long as European history continues to be written and read, but there were quite recent years when nothing seemed to be happening. More than thirty years ago the writer had completed some special studies in the Reformation period, and turned from them to his own sober unexciting duties with a sense of regret that his lot had not been cast in the great days. Then he read a valuable chapter in George Adam Smith's *Book of the Twelve Prophets* entitled " In the Midst of the Years " (vol. ii. 149), in which he comments on the use of that phrase in Habakkuk (iii. 2). The prophet has been recalling the magnificent deeds of the Lord in the days of the Exodus and his own age looks dull by contrast. " We, too, live amid the nameless years, " wrote G. A. Smith; " we feel them about us, undistinguished by the manifest workings of God, slow and petty, or, at the most, full of inarticulate turmoil ". Those very years, however, were critical in the sense that they were accumulating the material for the explosion that we called the Great War—but it didn't look like that to us !

In our judgments of others, we may well apply this principle. His subordinates suffered much from the capricious irritability of a master whose ill-temper they were afterwards able to trace to incessant and incurable pain. Perhaps the marvel was that he ever retained any self-control, and in so far as he did so, he achieved victory—but it didn't look like that to the sufferers ! There is usually a cause, if not a reason, for conduct which we deem hurtful and wrong, but we look on from the outside and our picture is inadequate.

Equally mistaken may be our view of ourselves and our work. In Christian service there are long periods of seemingly unheroic devotion to uninteresting tasks. The work of God up and down our land is maintained by faithful people who plod along, sticking to causes that have no semblance of grandeur. These hidden faithfulnesses are part of the victorious warfare of the Lamb. You, the local preacher, as you trudge along the road to your appointment, think loftily, though not proudly, of your business. Your journey is really necessary; your appointment is with the people of God, with the word of God, with the Incarnate Word of God ! You, the Sunday-school teacher, plodding to and fro between class and home, are partaking in the fulfilment of St. Paul's declaration; " The God of peace shall bruise Satan under your feet shortly ". Your treading the path of duty is part of that bruising of the enemy, even if it doesn't look like that to you ! When the enthroned Lord in the great Judgment Parable (Matt. xxv. 31-46) thanked His people for ministering to Him in sickness, in homelessness, in hunger and in imprisonment, were they not greatly surprised ? Did any of them say, " It didn't look like that to me " ?

There is an amazing estimate by our Lord in Luke x. 18. Seventy evangelists had traversed a country no larger than

Wales for a period unspecified but presumably not very long; they came back filled with enthusiasm over the results they had witnessed; even the supernatural forces of evil were subject to them in the name of their Lord ! When, however, we set the mission in the light of its context and the subsequent happenings, it does not appear quite so successful. The effect in many cases was temporary, and the Master Whose name cowed the demons was rejected and crucified by His own people. Even in the narrative of the return of the Seventy the notes of apparent failure are heard when Jesus speaks of the fact that certain things have been hidden from " the wise and prudent ", the intelligent people who count for most in the formation of public opinion. If we had been lookers-on, what judgment should we have passed on that campaign ? Not a very impressive one, probably. Yet our Lord says of it, in effect : " While you were preaching, I was watching something, someone ! I was looking at Satan (not *falling*, but) *fallen* from heaven "—not slowly sinking, but utterly prostrate ! The picture is not that of a parachutist gradually descending, but of a slain Goliath with a David (" great David's greater Son ") standing over him ! Now, with all the far greater Christian witness of to-day, yet the vaster apparent prosperity of evil, does it seem like that to you? Yet who can doubt that our Lord's view is the right one. He has the inside viewpoint.

What does the Christian conflict look like to " the glorious company of heaven " as they view it from the eternal world ? Here we must observe reverently the necessary limitations of our knowledge concerning the extent of their knowledge. Is it complete or partial ? The one statement upon which we can surely venture is that it must be of such a nature as that it will not cloud the felicity of those who are " with Christ ". Newman, in " Lyra Apostolica ", attributes to the Church Triumphant complete knowledge, using the Apocalyptic metaphor of " the sea of glass " :

> A sea before
> The Throne is spread; its pure still glass
> Pictures all earth-scenes as they pass.
> We on its shore
> Share, in the bosom of our rest,
> God's knowledge, and are blest !

That borders on the fanciful, and is unauthorised by any Scriptural warrant. Yet it does not seem presumptuous to think that these who are still fellow-members with us in the Church of Christ recall their warfare, and revise their earthly judgments on many an event. Triumphs are now apparent, where " it didn't seem like that " to those who were fighting a hard battle; what once wore the guise of a Divine withholding is now seen to have been God's way of giving " some better thing " to His people.

Do we sufficiently think of those " spirits of the just made perfect " ? Admittedly, Christian thought has been right in concentrating its mind on the Heavenly Lord rather than on the heavenly company, yet we may have played into the hands of the Spiritualists by our paucity of reference to the departed believers, who have still a most real life. There are dangers in an excessive use of the imagination concerning them, but equally there are dangers in the avoidance of the topic. It is right to ask, " What must it be to be there ? "— but when we arrive in the King's presence, we shall find all our anticipations marvellously and blessedly outdone, and looking back upon our expectations, and comparing the inside view with the outside, we shall say, " It didn't look like that to me ! "

XXIII

THE ART OF ASKING QUESTIONS

In his book called *The Philosophy of the Good Life*, Bishop Gore wrote: " I remember visiting Edward Caird on his death-bed in the Master's Lodge at Balliol, and finding him reading St. Augustine's *Confessions*; and he said to me, ' Whatever philosophers may say about this man's answers, at any rate he knew how to ask the right questions ' ". Edward Caird was himself eminent as a philosopher, and what is the study of philosophy except the putting of the all-important questions to the universe? He knew the value of the right question, and there is no place where proper questioning is more important than on a death-bed—though it ought not to wait till we come there !

The principal task of any teacher, in the home, in the Bible-class, in private discussion or wherever he may be exercising his teaching vocation, is to get his pupils to put to him the right questions; that is more important than any questions he may put to them ! Is there anything more lovely than a child's question? How much we learn when through their interested queries we can see the impression our familiar world is making upon a fresh and unspoilt mind ! Whenever we read the verse " Thou renewest the face of the earth ", we should think of the children we know and love, and of the springtime their coming makes in the heart and in the mind. Do you ever store up their questions? It is very wasteful to let their unconsciously wise sayings slip out of memory. A little child, born to the comfort and beauty that wealth can procure, was taken as a " short cut " through part of a London slum. He gazed on the squalor and suffering with shocked eyes, and then said to his nurse, " Does God know about this ? " How would you answer the question? But before you start to search for right answers, ask yourself whether it is a question you have ever put ? " Is there knowledge with the Most High ? " (Ps. lxxiii. 11) is probably to be understood in a similar sense; evil was prospering, and men wondered whether God knew about it. Well, He does know about it, and takes action about it ! For proof, consider

7

Ex. ii. 24, 25: " God heard their groaning, God remembered His covenant . . . God saw the children of Israel and God took knowledge of them ". " He careth for you ", Peter says; that is the right answer to this perfectly right question, but we shall only be in the right mood to hear the answer if we take the advice of Peter: " Casting all your care upon Him ".

Edward Caird praised Augustine for asking the right questions, so we spent some time (all too little !) turning over his wonderful *Confessions* to see what questions he asked. Here is one of them: " Is it then a slight woe to love Thee not ? " He tells of Victorinus, a secret disciple, a student of the Scriptures, who privately acknowledged to his friend that he was a Christian; the friend answered that he would not believe it until the secret disciple openly joined the Christian Church, whereupon Victorinus answered with a question, " Do walls then make Christians ? " Many different replies could be given to that question, for it can be understood in many different senses. If, however, we try to catalogue all Augustine's questions, a whole book will be needed; suffice it to say that our modern problems are nearly all present to him: the problem of evil, the mystery of the un-Christlike Church, the nature of God Himself, the difficulties of the Old Testament. He took questions on the latter point to Ambrose for solution, but was conscious that some of his questions were defences behind which he hid from the challenge of Christ. Have we any questions of that sort ? If so, let us put over against them a brave and noble word of that brave and noble believer, Tertullian: " God commands; why delay? "

Reverent imagination has often lingered over the record of the visit our Lord paid to the Temple in his twelfth year, especially the narrative of His mother finding Him there " in the midst of the teachers *both* hearing them *and* asking them questions ". Be sure to emphasise " both . . . and ". Behold the grace and condescension of Him Who is " the Wisdom of God ", yet Who listens to men as well as interrogates them ! All through the earthly ministry we see this considerateness, this approachableness, on the part of Christ; there are apparent exceptions, it is true, but rightly understood they confirm the picture. Sometimes " none of them durst ask Him any question " because His clear yet unchallengeable words had silenced them, or because the awe that filled their souls locked their lips. One flippant questioner, Herod, put idly curious questions to Him " but He answered him nothing ". We know the reason for that, and realise that such incurable shallowness of mind could receive nothing but the stern rebuke of Divine silence.

In the main, however, Christ encourages men to question Him, and there is much to be learnt from the way in which He handles the enquirers and their enquiries—notice the distinction, for sometimes it is truer to say that our Lord answers the questioner than the question ! When Peter puts a question about another disciple's future lot, Jesus dismisses the irrelevancy and recalls Peter to his own duty by saying: " What is that to thee ? Follow thou me ! " Again, when His followers ask the question which so many of us have longed to hear answered : " Lord, are there few that be saved ? ", our Master gives the only reply that would really be useful to anyone by saying : " Strive to enter in at the strait gate ". From speculative interest about the race as a whole we are recalled to our own need and opportunity.

Having referred to the questions that children put, let us draw two further lessons from them. Beware of questions that are big and vague ! A five-year-old boy once asked, " What is everything made of ? " Fortunately, he answered his own question by saying, " Work, I suppose ! " Some of the posers that clever unbelief puts are really unanswerable, such queries, for instance, as demand that we dwellers in time should explain eternity, or those which require that a limited human mind should be furnished with a complete and detailed account of God, the Omnipotent, Omniscient and Omnipresent. In a railway train a child asked her father as they went into a tunnel : " Why do they put hills on the tops of tunnels ? " An upside-down question ! But when we ask why God does not give us this, that or the other thing we have probably inverted our question. Here is the proper form : " Why should I keep one precious thing from Thee, when Thou hast given Thine own dear self for me ? "

Be careful of the *order* of your questions. It is important to ask " What ? " before " Why ? " and last of all we should ask " How ? " My meaning is that our first concern is with the actual fact, and only when we have made sure of that are we entitled to seek the reason for it. Anselm's famous book has a most necessary question for its title, *Why did God become man ?*, but it would do us no good to ask that question unless we were assured of the marvellous happening. Without despising such answers as we can find to the question " Why ? " we ought always to remember that the Gospel is first of all an announcement of certain great events, not an explanation of the causes of them. Paul delivered unto the Corinthian Church a statement of facts (1 Cor. xv. 3-8)—facts which can be to some extent reasoned about and supported by argument but which, in their full significance, are " a depth where all our thoughts are drowned ". Postpone " Why ? " to " What ? " therefore, and most carefully keep watch lest intrusive, assertive " How ? " pushes forward into too prominent a position ! Notice how Nicodemus was held in the fascination of " How ? " " How can these things be ? " " How ? . . . How ? " Our Lord's reply does not discuss the method of Divine action but asserts the reality of it, and calls Nicodemus back from " How ? " to " What ? " " We speak *what* we know and testify *what* we have seen ! "

We cannot ask the right questions unless we are willing ourselves to be questioned—in the right way and by the right person. Recollect how our Master dealt with men who dodged His questions: " Neither tell I you ! " (Matt. xxi. 23-27). The *spirit* of the questioner is all-important. And equally important is the *result* of the question. What shall we do when we have received the answer ? Speculate further about it, or act upon it ? The enquirer who asked: " Who is my neighbour ? " received an answer in the Parable of the Good Samaritan, but our Lord was not content to leave the man with nothing but an interesting and instructive story ; He challenged his judgment and reason by yet another question : " Which was neighbour to him that fell among thieves ? " (Luke x. 36). Then He followed up the questioner's reply with the command : " Go, and do thou likewise ! "

If you have a question that is serious, sincere and important, " Take it to the Lord in prayer ". But when the answer comes, act upon it ! Otherwise you will be a mere trifler, not one who asks the right questions.

XXIV

HIS TENT BESIDE MINE !

" THE Word became flesh, and *tabernacled* among us ".
What an interesting word " tabernacled " is ! It is full of
associations for the Bible-reader, and comes to us from the
speech of a people who had been tent-dwellers and could
never forget tent-life. Every year they celebrated the Feast
of Tabernacles, leaving their more substantial dwellings and
spending days in frail shelters, that they might recall the
wilderness days and the movable habitations which, for all
their temporary nature, were a protection from the burning
sun and the desert storm. Tents were more easily erected
than houses, but the Israelite learnt that the essential matter
was not the fabric of his dwelling-place but the blessing of
God upon it. " Except the Lord build the house, they labour
in vain that build it ! " And if the Lord's blessing is upon
the fragile tent, it is as safe as the strong fortress !
There was not only the private tent of the Israelite pilgrim,
but also the central Tent, the sacred Tabernacle, standing in
the midst of the encampment, the centre of the company
because the God for Whose worship it was set up was central
in the life of the people. The time came when the Temple
replaced the Tabernacle. It was fitting that the permanent
should take the place of the temporary, and that when Israel's
king dwelt in a house of cedar the Ark of God should no
longer dwell " between curtains ". Yet it was good for Israel
to look back from time to time to those days when worship
under simpler conditions was nevertheless crowned by evidence
of God's acceptance. There is spiritual gain sometimes in
forsaking the costly Temple for the simple Tent. Will the
destruction of some stately houses of worship bring as com-
pensation the recovery of a simplicity and earnestness that
finds the Divine presence in unpretending surroundings, and
knows that, since the Lord is in that place, it is none other than
the House of God, the very gate of heaven ?
Our associations with the word " Tabernacle " to-day are

7*

strangely different from those the Jew entertained. Loved and honoured structures, commodious and meant to be permanent, have borne the name; Spurgeon's Tabernacle is the example that occurs first to the mind, but it had many predecessors. We wonder why the name was selected. C. H. Spurgeon and his people were, of course, well aware that the word meant " tent ", and they must have had strong reasons for attaching an apparently inappropriate title to their sanctuary. Was it associated in their minds with White-field's Tabernacle in Moorfields, where in the middle of the eighteenth century evangelism had one of its strongholds, and did the choice of the name signify a desire to provide another centre where men would be addressed as sinners and urged to seek salvation from sin and sin's consequences ? It may be that Spurgeon and his people felt that " Church " should be kept for a company of redeemed people (which is correct), that " Temple " recalled a house of prayer that had become a den of thieves, so they chose " Tabernacle " as the remaining Biblical description. It is not a vital matter ! Meeting-house, Room, Tabernacle, Temple, Chapel or Church—whatever the name, what matters supremely is the Divine Presence. If that is withdrawn, it is no longer called by our Lord " My house ", but " *your* house ", and it is left unto us desolate.

Here, however, we would draw attention to the " tent " meaning contained in the word " tabernacle ". The verb " tabernacle " had been widened in use till it stood for a hut, a hovel, a workshop or a cottage, as well as an actual tent; there is even evidence of the word signifying a ship's cabin ! Through all these varying meanings there lingers the original sense of a dwelling that is simple, insubstantial and transitory. It is still a traveller's word, as the employment of it for a ship's cabin shows; how interesting it is, therefore, that Paul, the tent-maker, should compare his body to a tent ! At this point, though, my concern is with the choice of the word to describe the coming of our Lord, the Word made flesh, Who came and " tabernacled among us ".

That rendering is not quite adequate, yet, not as literal translation, but as a paraphrase to suggest the fuller meaning, let us express it thus: " He pitched His tent for a season among ours ". " For a season "—the days of His flesh were numbered and limited; true, when He took our nature into union with His own glorious divine nature He assumed it for ever, and is now and eternally fully Man as well as fully God, but the earthly humiliation was temporary; it was a road through a deep valley, in very truth a valley of the shadow of death; He passed through it and regained the heights of His glory, but He left the shadowed road less shadowed for all His people who follow after Him.

That temporary tent-life of our Incarnate Lord was a life at close quarters with ours ! We wonder where the tent of Joshua stood in relation to the tents of his soldiers when the Israelite army encamped over against Jericho; probably the general's tent would be removed from the rest, and given some place of seclusion, comfort, eminence and honour. But Christ, the Captain of the Lord's host, pitched His tent among ours ! Nay, let us make it yet more individual—*He pitched His tent beside mine!* Does the changed phrase make more vivid to our imagination the nearness of the Lord Jesus to men in our human condition ? If the uncertainties of life to-day make us feel that earth gives but a passing shelter and that the bodily life is a tent, not a fixed dwelling, then let us remember two things: One is that our Saviour Himself shared this condition, when His tent was pitched among those of mankind, and the other memorable thing is that He has gone to prepare for us who " dwell in tents " a sure abiding-place (John xiv. 2). This contrast between the seemingly unsettled life and the certainty of the promised inheritance underlies the great word about Abraham in Heb. xi. 9, 10. " By faith he became a sojourner in the land of promise, as in a land not his own "—living like an alien in a land that was his by right of God's gift—" dwelling in tents, with Isaac and Jacob, the heirs with him of the same promise "— as a mere visitor instead of resident proprietor, and this state of things endured through the lives of his son and grandson ! What enabled him to do that and yet not to doubt the promise ? Why, faith, and the vision that faith gains of the eternal and immovable: " He looked for the city which hath *the* foundations " (*i.e.* the true and lasting divine foundations, which are only found in the city " whose builder and maker is

God ". Notice that " builder " is rendered in the Revised Version margin " architect "; that heightens the meaning. Our structures are often less perfect than they might be because designer and constructor are not in complete harmony, or misunderstand each other; where the same Divine Worker is both architect and builder the design will be perfect and its execution complete !

He Who comes near to us in the Incarnation, placing His tent among ours, came still nearer to our need in His Cross. There we see not merely sympathy, but identification, for He was " made sin " for us. And that identification is no merely temporary matter; it includes a union that time and death cannot break. Beyond the changes and uncertainties of time we have the promise of being " for ever with the Lord ". Remembering how He tabernacled among us, let us receive afresh in faith the word: " Behold, the tabernacle of God is *with* men " (a closer union than " among men "), " and He shall dwell with them, and they shall be His people, and God Himself shall dwell with them and be their God ".

XXV

AN EASTER JOURNEY

THE first chapter in this volume ended with the suggestion—
rather an imaginative one !—that the comrade who went with
Cleopas to Emmaus on the first Easter Day was named
Phurah. We were not embroidering the narrative of Luke,
but suggesting that this unnamed fellow-traveller was Phurah
by disposition, whatever his legal name may have been.
There has always been interested discussion about his companion's identity; sometimes Cleopas has been identified
with the Clopas mentioned in John xix. 25, whose wife Mary
stood beneath the Cross of our Lord; then Mary was thought
to be accompanying her husband to Emmaus, which would
introduce a woman into the story. Unfortunately, the
identification of the two names is impossible, for, though
they are so near in sound and spelling, the one comes from
Aramaic and the other from Greek. In reality, they are quite
different names. Why did Luke introduce a name at all?
Some writers think that it is to indicate his informant.
Certainly the historian sometimes mentions people by name
with no apparent reason, unless it be to show that he had had
personal contact with actors in the scene, and is thus giving
first-hand information. As an example of this, notice his
reference to Joanna in Luke viii. 3 and xxiv. 10; nearly thirty
years ago Dr. Holdsworth called attention to " the intimate
knowledge shown (by Luke) of incidents connected with the
court of Herod ", and suggested that the source of this knowledge was Joanna, the wife of Herod's steward. As a medical
man, Luke would be able to converse more freely with women
than other men would. We are told that Herod said to his
servants, " This is John the Baptist ". Was Joanna's husband
one of those servants, was his interest in John the Baptist
quickened, did he communicate that interest to his wife, did
she look beyond the Forerunner to the One to Whom he
pointed as " the Lamb of God ", did she abandon the court
of Herod to serve the King of Kings, did service for Him in

later days bring her into touch with Luke, and was it thus that he learnt and recorded for us facts which otherwise must have been forgotten ? It is a long chain of supposition, but contains no improbabilities, and those who believe that God can and does link together previously unconnected lives to form the chain of His purposes will find here nothing incredible but much cause for " wonder, love and praise ".

That is rather a digression, but we are thinking about travellers, so some wandering may be forgiven. It has been thought (we have said) that Cleopas is named by Luke because he was Luke's informant—but suppose that the other traveller gave the information ? And suppose that he had no desire for mention or prominence (like other Phurahs) and that he gave Luke the name of his comrade, Cleopas, but begged that his own name should be omitted ? It is merely supposition, but not impossible; if so, we can call the two men by name, Cleopas and Phurah ! Let us go with them to Emmaus !

We have no portrait that shows their features, but their expression is described, and sometimes that is more revealing than a portrait ! They looked " sad "—a highly expressive word, which we can perhaps understand by the fact that it is used in the Greek translation of Gen. xl. 7; " Wherefore look ye so sadly to-day ? " That is an excellent illustration, for it speaks of two men who had dreamed and then awakened, but could make no sense of their dream. Did Cleopas and his comrade feel that they had awakened from a dream which had no meaning ? Is there anything sadder ? Consider Macfadyen's rendering of Ps. lxxiii. 20: " Like a dream, when one awakes, shall they be, whose phantoms the waker despises ! " How good it is that " when I awake, I am still with Thee " (Ps. cxxxix. 18) ! That is what happened to these comrades. The One Who seemed to have been only a dream was a reality, and as they went along He came *hurrying behind them*. (That is involved in verses 14 and 18; He is coming from Jerusalem, and overtakes them). He is still the Good Shepherd, and when His sheep are likely to be scattered he eagerly goes forth in search of them, losing no time in His urgent quest.

Have you noticed the two instances of apparent discourtesy on the part of our Lord in this story ? One is in verse 17, when He asks to be told the subject of their conversation. Imagine a casual passer-by requiring to be told what it is that you and your friend are discussing ! Yet no resentment or even surprise was felt, for Cleopas at once gives the information; (Cleopas here, like Paul in Acts xiv. 12, was evidently " the chief speaker "; men of the Phurah tribe are often, like Moses, slow of speech !) Although the two friends had not yet recognised Jesus, they instinctively felt that He had a right to ask questions of a personal character that in any other case would have been deemed rude and intrusive. Have we fully recognised our Master's right to put every kind of question to us ? Are we prepared for His interrogation about our private conversation and our most secret deeds ? And do we accord Him a place of such pre-eminence that no enquiry of His can ever be judged out-of-place or unjustified ? What in others would be impertinence is His native right !

The other instance of apparent discourtesy is in verse 30, where He, the invited Guest, assumes as of right the place and function of the Host, and breaks the loaf. (Dalman has an interesting statement to the effect that in the East there are no thick loaves, so that no use of the knife was needed; moreover, " to the Orientals the application of a knife for the cutting of bread would have meant a violation of God's gift ".) Again, our Lord's assumption of an unusual authority is not resented by the two men; their eyes were still unopened, but already they knew that this Stranger must take the first place wherever He comes.

We have been anticipating, however; let us return to the wayfarers. Their unproductive debate is an emblem of much discussion in our own day; Christ's words in verse 17 suggest arguments and quotations " tossed to and fro ", like children playing at ball—an entertaining occupation, but not one that achieves great results ! When, however, the Divine Teacher enters into the conversation, the profitless debate becomes a gladdening revelation ! Previously, you see, Cleopas and Phurah had been holding a Bible Class—without the presence of their Lord ! If any reader of these words goes to a Bible Class next Sunday, may he find that where two or three, (Cleopas, Phurah and others) are gathered together, there Christ is in the midst.

Still, though He taught them so much, why did He keep them waiting for the full revelation ? He dealt with them very tenderly and graciously (" fools " in verse 25 simply means " unperceiving ones "), yet not till the close of the journey did He make His full disclosure—why ? Was it in order that their eyes might be slowly accustomed to growing light, not blinded by a sudden flash ? Or was it that they might be yet more sure of a conclusion gradually established in their minds than they would be of an intuition instantaneously gained ?

At any rate, the journey to Emmaus is more than past history; it has elements that are still repeated. Our Lord in this incident set the seal of His approval on " the fellowship of kindred minds ", yet showed that such fellowship without Him in the central and supreme position becomes only a saddening disputation. The Christian Church to-day is plodding rather wearily along the road; may the experience of Christ's presence give us all the burning heart ! Then we shall be like these tired travellers who, for all their weariness, could not rest till they spread the glad tidings !